Copyright © 2025 Tim Ewell.

All rights reserved. No part of this book may be reproduced, stored, or transmitted by any means—whether auditory, graphic, mechanical, or electronic—without written permission of both publisher and author, except in the case of brief excerpts used in critical articles and reviews. Unauthorized reproduction of any part of this work is illegal and is punishable by law.

ISBN: 979-8-89419-587-2 (sc)
ISBN: 979-8-89419-588-9 (hc)
ISBN: 979-8-89419-589-6 (e)

Because of the dynamic nature of the Internet, any web addresses or links contained in this book may have changed since publication and may no longer be valid. The views expressed in this work are solely those of the author and do not necessarily reflect the views of the publisher, and the publisher hereby disclaims any responsibility for them.

One Galleria Blvd., Suite 1900, Metairie, LA 70001
(504) 702-6708

Recon Airplane Company

III Corps, Vietnam

TIM EWELL

The book is dedicated to two very special friends and comrades in arms:

To Capt. Michael D. Lacross, always my best friend.

And to the memory of Mr. Christopher W. H. Beale, an English-born gentleman and American patriot.

Chapter 1

The sounds of gunfire were everywhere. Some were single shots, others were bursts of automatic fire. The boy could hear the crack of bullets as they broke the sound barrier overhead. Village women were screaming, and the invading men, dressed in what would appear to be silky black pajamas, were shouting as they moved quickly and deliberately from hut to hut. Over the noise of the Vietcong soldiers, their guns and the screams of the villagers, he could hear his mother's voice telling him to run, run fast, into the jungle. He felt her pushing him from behind.

He ran as fast as his short legs allowed down the narrow, winding path into the depths of the dark jungle. His mother's excited voice was still behind him, screaming, telling him to run faster. He kept running, not looking back, farther and farther into the misty, damp forest.

The sounds of the gunfire became less intense as he penetrated deeper into the shadows. Now, as he listened, they sounded like they were far away. He stopped for just a second to catch his breath and turned around. He was startled and frightened to find he was completely alone. He started to turn back, but something told him to hide and wait for his mother. Hiding was something he had done before. His mother had taught him how. It was like their special game. He knew the men in the black pajamas didn't like him, and they didn't like his mother either. He had to hide. He had to be very quiet. They must not find him. But where was his mother? She'd always been there before.

He hid behind a big leafy bush, almost invisible beneath its branches, and he waited, holding his breath and listening. He peeked between the branches and strained to see if his mother was coming. He listened intently for her voice. Where was she?

In the depths of this triple canopy jungle there was little light. Small rays of yellow sunlight penetrated here and there, like shining streaks of gold. But the sun was not a familiar visitor here. In the heat of this region of Southeast Asia, the dewy dampness of the jungle created a foggy mist. Where the little rays of light were able to pierce the dense umbrella of foliage, it made the mist sparkle like bright little fireflies.

After what seemed like forever to him, the sound of the gunfire ended. The voices in the distance faded and then died, and the jungle was quiet. A small gray monkey came out from behind a tree branch just above him, looked down at him, and then scurried higher into the lush jungle canopy, squealing as if to say, "I'm getting the heck out of here while I can."

He continued to listen, but it remained quiet. He decided that it would now be all right to leave his hiding place and to go back to find his mother. Carefully, he crawled out from his hiding place and started toward the almost invisible jungle path that led back to the village. He called for her, softly at first, then, a little louder. The sound of his voice was quickly absorbed by the dense undergrowth. He could see the narrow path was just ahead. He stepped toward it, slowly picking his way around a prickly jungle vine that grew alongside a tall rubber tree.

Suddenly, a black shadowy figure rose in front of him. He quickly turned to run back to the security of his hiding place, but before he could take two steps, a strong hand grabbed his arm and swung him around. The VC soldier looked at him. The boy lowered his head to avoid the soldier's eyes. The soldier barked at him to look up, and he slowly raised his head till he was looking right into the soldier's face. The man in black looked back. and the boy saw a look he'd seen before. The face of the soldier filled with hate, and he mumbled some words that were barely understandable. The boy struggled to escape the hands that held him captive, but the soldier's grip was too strong. The soldier shouted angry words at him, and he began to shake as tears filled his eyes. He was barely aware of the second presence moving up behind him. Suddenly something hard hit him in the back of the head. His legs went numb, and he fell face first, unconscious, onto the jungle floor.

The silk-clad soldiers exchanged words. They took the small limp body and dragged him off the path into the foliage a few yards and dropped him. He was nearly invisible underneath a large broad leafed plant.

* * *

They knew that Viet Cong had been out recruiting in the area. But trying to find them was like trying to find an elusive ghost. Most of the time, all you could do was find traces of where they had been. They were only an eight-man long-range patrol, and their mission was to find "Charlie," as the VC were called. Then they could bring in a larger force, maybe even an air strike, and destroy them.

The villagers hated soldiers, all soldiers—US, Vietcong, anyone in a uniform, whether black pajamas or green jungle fatigues—and that made the job harder. They did not want to talk to anyone. But who could blame them? For as long as most of them could remember, soldiers had destroyed their lives. Charlie would come in and take their male children from the age of ten or twelve and force them to become fighters like themselves. The French, and later the UN Forces, mainly Americans, would come into the village looking for Charlie, and end up destroying most of the village, sometimes all of it. All these poor farmers really wanted was to be left alone to grow their rice and vegetables and raise their families. But it was not to be—at least not yet.

Lt. Johnson had decided to sweep around to the east side of the village and clear the flank before going in to check out the village status. It was a classic maneuver, a necessary one to make sure they wouldn't be ambushed. The entire patrol was alert because they'd met a scattered force of VC earlier in the day. They'd shot and killed two, but several got away. Spec Four Manx had taken a hit in the leg, but he was still doing okay. The wound was pretty much a through-and-through and hadn't done a lot of damage. It was bandaged tight, and the bleeding had stopped. He had a little limp, but that was about it. They were due at LZ (Landing Zone) Whiskey tomorrow at 0900, and Manx would be fine till then.

Sgt. Britman was on point. He knew that the deep jungle can be your friend at times, and at other times your deadly enemy. If you're good, it can hide you well and you can sneak up on your adversary. If the opposition is good, it can hide them well too. Britman's job was to lead the way, being careful not to step on a mine or catch a trip wire. He was good at his job, and he was always thinking ahead.

He looked before he stepped. His eyes swept back and forth and up and down, looking for any hint of danger, be it wire or a mine. Cautiously, he made his way through the thick underbrush. He moved stealthily until his foot caught on something, and he lost his balance and fell forward. In his mind he was thinking, *This isn't right*, and his instincts for survival quickly took over.

"You okay, Brit?" came the hushed voice from a few feet behind him.

Britman started to struggle to his feet, that uncertain feeling still in the back of his head, and answered back that all was fine, But as he tried to regain his balance, his hand felt the warmth of a body beneath him. He froze. "Smitty, get over here quick, at the ready," he said in a loud whisper, more anxious than usual.

Cpl. Johnny Smith, tall and dark skinned, with camouflage grease paint on his face, held up his hand and made a fist to give the signal to the rest of the team to stop. He gripped his M16 in his right hand, crouched down, and slowly made his way toward the anxious voice.

A few careful steps and he was there. "Brit, what the h—" He looked at Britman, whose face was pale. He was frozen in an arch over top of a small figure face down hidden in the foliage.

"Help me up," said Britman.

Smitty set his rifle down off to his right side, still in easy reach if needed, and reached out to grab the back of Britman's jungle fatigue jacket. He pulled up while Britman rocked back on his heels to stand up. But he did not stand up all the way. He kept one hand firmly on the back of the warm body below him, making sure it could not move.

By now three more of the team members had cautiously caught up to the point man. Lt. Johnson was the fourth to arrive. "What's going on?" he whispered.

Britman stood, looking down at the small body lying nearly undetectable in the green shadows below him. He took several quick deep breaths. "Satchel. Could have a satchel charge," he muttered in a low whisper.

One of a point man's major fears was to stumble over a land mine or snag a trip wire. A good point man was always looking for such booby traps. But the body trick was famous. Charlie would take a dead soldier—ours or theirs, it didn't matter to them—and rig the body with explosives. Then they'd leave it in such a way that an unsuspecting soldier would have to roll the body over to investigate—and "BOOM," one less GI. This patrol knew the trick well. It had only been three weeks since they'd lost a careless newbie in a similar ploy. Britman had been on a two-day leave, and it had left him extra aware of his surroundings. Hell, it could have been him, and he knew it. He had to drum such thoughts out of his mind, or he could never do his job.

Beneath him, the little boy thought he heard strange voices in the back of his mind, like they were whispering nearby. It was kind of like an echo. He started to move, but it was like everything was a dream and he just couldn't wake up.

"So what do we do now?" whispered Britman, not yet aware that there was life in the little body.

Lt. Johnson made his way over to where Britman was standing. "Well, for one thing, you three take up positions. Charlie might be watching just to find out what we do. And if this kid's wired, we don't need to have four of us blown up."

The other three spread out and made a semicircle facing outward, weapons at the ready. The rest of the team was given the hand signal to go defensive on the other side. Lt. Johnson looked down. "He can't be more than five or six years old."

"And he's breathin'," noted Britman in an anxious whisper as he felt the boy's lungs fill with air.

"Hey, they wouldn't satchel a live one, would they?" asked Johnson.

"Dunno, El Tee. You know these guys are nuts and they—he's movin'!" Britman said excitedly.

In the child's mind, he could hear his mother's voice telling him to run. *Run away from soldiers. Hide in jungle.* He had to get up and get away. Using all the effort he could muster, he started to struggle to his feet, but then he felt the firm hand of the big spec 4 push him back down.

"Step back, El Tee—he could blow," Britman said softly.

Caught off guard by the almost gentle words, Johnson took a quick step backward. As he did, he could see Brit sliding his hand under the boy, feeling around like he was looking for something. He stopped his retreat and moved back alongside his point man, who was now kneeling beside the boy.

"I think were okay, Sir. No wires, no charges."

"And if there were, you'd be dead by now," said the lieutenant.

"Just felt like a chance worth takin', Sir."

They both took a deep breath. Then Johnson said, "Well, let's see what we've got."

Britman took hold of a little arm and turned the boy over. Almost providentially, a single ray of light pieced through the jungle and shone on the boys face just as he opened his eyes. Britman let out an unexpected gasp. "He's a round eye," he said in astonishment, "a blue-eyed round eye."

"Well I'll be . . ."

The little boy was awake now, but his head was still fuzzy. He didn't know what was happening, but these were men with guns. That meant soldiers, and that meant trouble. *Where is my mother?* he thought. *I need to find my mommy.* He struggled to get free, but Britman's grip was strong.

"El Tee, look at this." said Britman as he drew one hand away from the boy. "Blood! The kid's bleeding. We better get Doc to take a look at him."

Johnson nodded and signaled for the team medic. Doc drew back from his position on the makeshift perimeter and joined them. "Whatcha got, Sir?"

"Young kid, looks like a half breed. He's bleedin'. Do what you can and hurry. We've been here too long." It almost went without saying that they all knew they had to keep moving. Staying in one place too long when you were unsure of your surroundings was a sure way to end up in the middle of a firefight.

"Yes, Sir," Doc replied. The little boy continued to struggle, to get away from what he knew was real trouble. But he'd lost a lot of blood, and his efforts made him dizzy again. He passed out in Britman's strong arms.

The team continued their sweep, and as they did they came upon another still body. They found it about a hundred yards up the path from where they'd found the boy. She was lying on her back. Taller than most Vietnamese women they'd seen, she was strikingly beautiful—even in death. They wondered what the connection to the boy might be. They left her body there because they were not that far from the village, and they knew she would be found and taken care of in the traditional customs of this culture. They were too vulnerable to let their presence be known, and they didn't need to be carrying around more dead weight. It was just what was practical and necessary to preserve life on a mission like this.

The next day, as the UH-1 Huey choppers lifted off from LZ Whiskey, they had an extra team member on board. His head was bandaged with a white field dressing that was stained red. Britman held him close as he slept. The rest of the team, in a protective mode, kept a watchful eye on him. They flew back to Phu Loi without incident and landed inside the perimeter.

Once on the ground, Britman carried his newfound charge to his hooch like he was just another duffle bag. No one outside the team took notice—not the pilots, not the crew chief, not the ground handlers. It was just another hot, humid day in what had once been a true paradise but was now what seemed like a place of ongoing torment. It was just another LRRP team—Long Range Reconnaissance Patrol, or "lerp," when spoken—coming home from a couple weeks in the field. This time they all made it back alive. This time there was a special bonus.

Chapter 2

(Sung to the tune of "Sweet Betsy from Pike")

♫ *Oh Phu Loi, Oh Phu Loi, a hell of a place,*
This organizations a fucking disgrace,
With captains and majors and light colonels too,
With thumbs up their asses with nothing to do.

They rant and they rave and they cuss and they shout.
They profess to know what they know nothing about.
For the good that they're doing they might as well be,
Shoveling shit on the South China Sea. ♫

The little Officers' Club was full of lively RAC pilots. They sang their songs, joked about how silly some of their assignments were, and somehow all the things that they dealt with on a day-to-day basis were just a little better. After all, who could they blame for being so far away from home in a country where it seemed that no one wanted them? Back home, the mood was that it was a bad war and that the US should be out of it. Young men were burning their draft cards and moving to Canada. There's no such thing as an easy war, but this one was worse than most.

Every war had its patriotic songs. WWI had "Over There," a rousing little ditty about how important it was to get in and get the job done. "And we won't come back till it's over, over there," George M. Cohan had written that one. WWII also had its share of patriotic tunes, and the American people loved and supported their heroes.

The Vietnam War had its songs too, but most of what anyone remembers are a few songs about how worthless it all was. One particular song that seemed to have universal appeal was dearly loved by all the men serving in Vietnam. It was the Animals singing, "We gotta get out of this place, if it's the last thing we *ever* do . . ."—and for many, it was the last thing they ever did. And to those serving in 'Nam, it seemed that few ordinary citizens back home were showing their support for the war—or the troops who'd been asked to serve their country. Those who'd been drafted had no choice.

This sentiment of the general US populace was out of character with how most of this group of officers felt. They were told they were there to halt the spread of communism and to keep other countries from falling, one after the other—the domino theory, as it was known. These officers were all patriotic Americans who felt there was a job they'd been called on to do, and that they were going to do it as best they could. Well, almost all of them felt that way—at least that's what they said. Even the few who really wanted to get out of the war zone as fast as they could at least believed that the war had meaning. They assumed that someone in Washington, who obviously had more information than they did, had sent them here for a reason. They just had to trust that it was a good one.

What was generously called the Officers' Club was just a large room at the end of the Officers' Quarters. Over the last couple of years, the pilots who came and went as they filled their tour of duty had built a bar. The base of the bar was made of standard-sized red bricks, over which was laid a sheet of plywood covered with polyurethane. From one end to the other, the whole thing curved forming a sort of lazy "S." There were short bar stools on the customer side, and the back side had been dug out and a lower cement floor had been poured. The end result? When someone was standing behind the bar, they were about eye level with those who were seated on stools.

And what a group of men they were, gathered there that night in the room at the end of the barracks.

"Terry" said Pop in a loud voice as Terry entered the room. "Over here!"

"Pop" Danforth, was a WWII B-29 tail gunner retread who was now a Cessna Bird Dog pilot, age unknown but believed to be about forty-eight. He was also know as the company scrounge. He was at the bar and motioned for Terry to come over to the open stool between he and Billy. Billy "The Kid" Williamson, the youngest at nineteen, a blond-haired, blue-eyed handsome kid with an outspoken nature, a big ego, and a rather obvious lack of maturity.

"Hey, Terry" said Billy. "Ready for a cold one."

Terry sat down on the stool. "So you're telling me we had enough power to run the refrigerator today? Will wonders never cease?"

"Well sort of" answered Pop. "It's certainly on the cold side of warm."

Terry took a quick look around the room. There in his usual place was Captain Ralph Horse a full-blooded Hopi Indian who was already a minor legend because of some of his flying exploits—like when he was flying low-level and enemy fire shot out his aileron cables, and he flew back to base and landed his little O-1 Bird Dog with only rudder and elevator control. Ralph was sitting at the green felt-covered poker table at the back of the room, and as always had the largest stack of chips on the table.

"Your gonna bet or what." Terry heard him say to Major Randolph who was sitting across from him. Major Randolph, was an interesting character in his own right. He had been known to bite a chunk off of his drinking glass, chew it up, and swallow it. He would do it on a dare, or just to get attention.

"Patience, my man, patience," said Randolph peeking at his cards one more time.

"It's not like we don't have all night" said Bart Nelson.

Captain Bart "Nude" Nelson was a real a-typical army officer. He spent most of his time on the base walking around buck naked except for his flip-flop sandals. He was a little overweight, and felt he stayed cooler that way. He didn't care who was around or where he was going, he was always as out of uniform as possible—even sans underwear. The hooch maids who tended to the laundry and cleaning the rooms would shriek when they saw him walking down the hall, but he never gave it a second thought. Tonight at least, he had on his green army fatigue pants.

"If I could get a decent hand, maybe this would be a game," said Don Milford as he pushed away from the poker table and headed for the bar.

He was the one pilot most out of character. He was the chubby Captain Donald "Mile High" Milford. He got the nickname because he rarely flew his aircraft in a manner to put himself in any danger. The higher he flew, the safer he felt, so he flew his Bird Dog above 5,000 feet most of the time—a mile high. It really pissed off the observers who were assigned to fly with him, who wanted to get down on the deck and see things close-up. Behind his back, a lot of the guys called him "Major" Milford because he was always acting like he was in charge. The other guys learned to look out for themselves when they were around him because he was known to report what he thought was inappropriate behavior to the "old man"—the CO—and then they'd have some explaining to do. That could be tedious. Milford just didn't fit in with the rest of the guys.

But no matter their differences, their sacred bond was their shared love of flying.

Even though the Eighty-ninth Reconnaissance Airplane Company (RAC) was technically operational twenty-four hours a day, evenings brought the pilots together in the club for some relaxation. It was a time to tell stories about the day's missions, a time to play cards or challenge a friend to a game of liar's dice and have a drink—hopefully paid for by the other guy, when he lost. It seemed one thing pilots did a lot of was drink. Only a few stayed away from it, usually because they were serious about being the best at their job they could be. One or two didn't drink because—well, they just didn't. For them it was either a religious or a personal conviction. There was only one time when it became a problem for the non-drinkers, and that time was tonight.

It was "Flamin' Mamie" time.

"Hey, Saunders—get over here," shouted Captain MacDillard as he got up and headed for the bar.

Saunders looked up from a table in the center of the room, where he was talking to a couple of fellow pilots, and saw MacDillard sitting down at the bar just as the bar tender placed a bottle of Drambuie on the bar in front of him. He saw a certain gleam in MacDillard's eye and quickly sized up the situation. "That's okay, Sir, I'd rather not," he said politely. He quickly glanced at the door to see if he could make a tactful retreat. He picked up the sweating can of Coke in front of him and shot another glance at the exit.

"Did you hear what I said, Lieutenant Newbie? Get over here," MacDillard commanded in a loud, bullying voice. He pulled out his Colt 45 semi-automatic pistol and aimed it at the ceiling as if poised to fire.

"Mac, not again!" shouted Major Randolph. "We still have a leak in the roof from the last time. Saunders, get up to the bar and get it over with."

Mac lowered the pistol and put it back in it's holster.

Well, now I'm stuck, thought Saunders. He slowly pushed away from the table and walked over to MacDillard. Mac didn't impress anyone with his size, and he had the attitude of a small man. He had to impress with his rank, which wasn't all that impressive. He often appeared angry and demanding. He had few friends, and it was not hard to see why. He was a bully.

Lt. Bill Saunders was no small fry. At six foot and 190 pounds, and not too many months out of OCS, he was in really good shape. On a level playing field, Mac would be in trouble. But Mac had rank. He had power over lieutenants.

"Yes, Sir," said Saunders without enthusiasm. He'd almost resigned himself to the situation, and in his mind he thought, *Well if it happens, at least that will be the end of it.*

"It's your turn. You're a newbie around here, and you have a duty to prove yourself, just like everyone else." MacDillard turned to the short warrant officer behind the bar. "Prepare the potion," he said with glee.

Saunders thought he would give it one more try. "I really don't care to take part in your hazing ritual, if you don't mind, Sir, and I don't recall anything about this . . . duty, as you call it, in any manual I've ever read." He was respectful, yet dismissive.

"I don't care what you don't care, Lieutenant. Get ready for your initiation." MacDillard's voice was harsh and commanding. "And it's not hazing—it's tradition."

Saunders took a deep breath and pondered the situation. He felt his heart start to beat harder. His palms began to sweat. He really preferred to get out of this. But how could he? All his friends had left their tables and were gathered around the bar to watch the show. Even Ralph Horse put down his poker hand and got up from his game, and very little got Ralph away from a poker game. The other three players joined him including the XO, Randolph. Now it made him feel like it was a sanctioned event so he might as well give in to the inevitable.

The newbie felt a little sick to his stomach. He'd watched others as they'd undergone the ordeal. It was an almost impossible task, and the only result was to make the new guy very drunk and probably very sick. He really wasn't ready for either. The obnoxious Captain MacDillard was to his right. Mac often drank too much, and tonight . . . . he'd outdone himself.

"Now, who'll give this new lieutenant a demonstration of how the 'Flamin' Mamie' works?" barked MacDillard.

A voice answered from right behind him. "I will, no sweat. It's easy. Just watch me," came the over-eager response. It was Captain Whitehead. Normally a quiet, shy sort of a guy, but on special nights like this he shined. His whole personality took on a special sparkle. It was probably because he was the best at proving the trick would work if it was done right. And he had the scar down the side of his neck that attested to at least one failed practice session.

"Go ahead, Whitey," said MacDillard, "show the lieutenant how it's done."

"Where's the fire marshal?" said Whitey as he looked at the officers standing nearest to him.

"Oh yeah, I almost forgot," said MacDillard. "Armanski, grab a glass full of water and stand by. You are hereby officially appointed fire marshal for the evening's festivities. You know what to do, don'tcha?"

Armanski was standing behind the bar. "Right," he said. "I've done this before." He reached for a glass and stuck it under the faucet, filled it with water, and set it on the bar in front of him.

"Now here's the rules," said MacDillard. "The shot glass is filled with Drambuie right up to the brim." He carefully filled the glass and checked to assure it was full. "Then we light it like this." He took a book of matches out of his shirt pocket, opened it up, and tore out a match. He struck the match and put it next to the edge of the glass. After a short second, the flame appeared. It was a blue flame that gently arched about an inch above the amber liquid.

"You ready, Whitey?" MacDillard asked.

Without hesitation, Whitey carefully gripped the glass between his thumb and fingers, gently lifted it to his mouth, being careful not to spill it, cocked back his head, and with a gentle twist of his wrist, poured the flaming contents into his open mouth. He shut his mouth, swallowed, smiled with satisfaction and pride, wiped his lips off with his tongue, and laughed. In the same fluid motion, he took the glass and slowly, gently, set it back on the bar. There was still a small flame arching delicately above the shot glass.

"Now here's the trick," said MacDillard. "When he set the glass down, the flame was still burning. That's a must. Now he has to pick it up and get at least one and no more than three drops to fall out."

Whitey picked up the glass and turned it carefully to pour out the remaining bit of liquor—one drop, two, and the flame went out. "And that's how I got the name, 'The Blue Flame,'" Whitey said with authority and pride. A cheer erupted from the crowd gathered at the bar. Whitey returned the glass to the table, stood up, and walked around to the back of the bar, where he could better watch the action to come.

"You see," said Mac, "easy, isn't it."

Saunders shuddered but held his emotions in check as he flashed a steely sneer at Mac. He'd heard a few stories about mustaches that had caught fire, and how Whitey got that burn scar on his neck. Apparently before his skills got really polished, he'd missed his mouth and the flaming liquor had run down his neck, and the fire marshal had reacted a little too slowly. But it was okay now. It was a bit like a scar of distinction. It was not unlike the days of swordsmen, when the teacher would carve a scar on the face of his student to signify the student had now become an accomplished fencer. Saunders wondered if he'd now bear the scar of a Mensur Master Drinker.

"Set it up," said Saunders disgustedly, now fully resigned to his fate. He sat down on the short bar stool next to Mac.

The drink was prepared. The flame was lit. Saunders lifted it carefully, his hand shaking a little. Ski picked up the water glass and stood ready to douse him, should it become necessary. Following Whitey's example, Saunders cocked back his head and poured the flaming contents down his throat , but as he returned the glass to the bar, he moved a little too quickly and the flame went out. The syrupy Drambuie was about the sweetest thing Bill had ever tasted, and not being a regular drinker, it burned his throat. He coughed.

"No good," cried MacDillard gleefully.

Arrogant bastard, thought Saunders. *I have nothing to prove to him.*

Saunders tried again, and again. Twenty minutes and six shots later, they accepted his efforts. Yes the group cheered, but he got no satisfaction out of it. With little emotion, a bit of relief, and some disgust, he got up from the chair, dismissed himself, and left the club, getting several pats on the back from his fellow pilots as he left. Outside, he held onto a post that held up the covered walkway. His head swirled and he bent over, and he knew what was coming. As the contents of his stomach spewed onto the ground, he began to feel better. He wiped his mouth on his sleeve, walked back into the bar, grabbed his now warm can of Coke, gave a mock salute to Mac, and walked out the door to go back to his room. He could hear the drunken MacDillard yelling at another new guy to repeat the performance. Saunders silently wished him luck.

At least that part's over, he thought. *Now I can get on with the serious stuff.* "Mac, you got one coming from me. Count on it," he mumbled as he walked back to his room.

* * *

After the other newbie had finished his initiation ritual, and Mac was passed out with his head on his folded arms on the bar, the remaining officers gathered once again in their little groups to play cards and exchange stories. Overhead could be heard the sound of Hueys and Chinooks coming and going. It was a twenty-four-hour war zone, and the night belonged to the enemy. But tonight they were relatively safe in their sandbag-

Tim Ewell

protected quarters. Tomorrow they'd be flying out in the open in enemy territory, risking their lives for the sake of "the mission." Tonight they could forget, pretend they were back home in some beer joint with their friends. For a little while, they could just relax.

Chapter 3

Barbara Armanski was a real beauty. She was a slim five-two with blond hair and a bright smile that could light up a whole room—and often did. The other officers' wives called her the "can-do kid" because she just had an uncanny ability to solve a problem or accomplish a task that seemed impossible to others. She said it was her positive outlook. "There's always hope," she would say firmly, "and where there's hope, there's possibility."

She and Steve had been married for three years. When they first met at UCLA, she was a senior studying nursing, and he was a junior studying engineering. He had a '64 1/2 Mustang convertible—red, of all colors, which gave him a reputation of being a little fast. They'd met at an off-campus party put on by one of her girlfriends. His date had wandered off halfway through the evening, disappeared with one of the football players, and he Barbara had ended up sitting across from each other at a small table discussing flying, his favorite subject. They just clicked.

A couple of dates and several fascinating conversations later, they both knew they were right for each other. "The way you two look at each other is almost sickening," her best friend told her. "God, I envy you."

That was late October of 1965. They were married in a beautiful garden wedding at Barbara's parent's home in Palo Alto just after Barbara graduated in June of 1966. Steve looked particularly handsome in his black tuxedo, and Barbara was exquisitely beautiful in her flowing white, lace-trimmed wedding dress. Her smile lit up the room, and when at the end they kissed, everyone knew it was the real thing. They seemed to be perfect for each other.

Barb planned to continue her education in pursuit of her nursing career. In the meanwhile she would get a part-time job in a local nursing home. She'd been interviewed, and her charm had easily won them over. She got the job, and after just a couple of days at work it seemed apparent that the staff was happy to have her. They really appreciated her enthusiasm and lust for life. They willingly welcomed her as a part of their group. The people she cared for were mostly elderly with little to look forward to. Barb made many of them smile just because of her upbeat attitude. They could tell she really cared. She had a gift.

Steve was planning to complete his senior year and go on to additional flight training from there. He already had a part-time job in a camera shop, his hobby doing photography was now paying some short-term dividends. The boss there told him that he'd be put on full-time for the summer. He and Barbara would save their money and trust that the future would match the grand plans and dreams that they shared.

They had pretty much settled into the little apartment. It was small, but it was what they could afford right now. Barbara was in the kitchen when Steve walked in the door, tossed the mail on the table, walked over to the refrigerator, and looked inside.

"Hey—that's not a TV set," said Barbara as he stared inside. "What are you looking for?" She picked up the mail and saw an envelope marked "Official Government Business." "What's this?"

"What's what?" answered Steve.

"This government letter. It's addressed to you."

"Heck if I know. I didn't look at the mail yet. Open it up if you're so curious."

Recon Airplane Company: III Corps, Vietnam

Barbara ripped off the end of the envelope and slid out the contents. She practically flopped down into the kitchen chair as she began to read. Steve heard her gasp and turned around. He caught her reaction as she turned white.

The words slapped her in the face: "Greetings from the President of the United States. You are hereby . . ."

It boiled down to this. He'd lost his student deferment. Because he wasn't taking summer classes, he was no longer considered an active student. He called everyone he could think of at every agency he could find, but there were just no loopholes for him. Yes, he was registered for the fall semester. Yes, he was married. And yes, he was not in school for the three months of summer. Therefore he was eligible for the draft and his number had been drawn. He even tried to enroll for summer classes, but it was too late.

He had no choice but to report for the required physical exam on the appointed date. When the morning dawned on that dreaded day, he was awake early. He talked to himself in the mirror as he shaved. "I'll just take it one day at a time. Something good is bound to come of this."

Barb overheard him and came into the rather cramped bathroom. She kissed his lathered cheek but said nothing. They'd said it all the night before. The possibility of ending up in that war called Vietnam was now a possibility. She gave him another kiss on the forehead, he felt the warmth of her body against him, and that familiar thrill ran up his spine. He looked in her eyes, gave her a kiss and patted her on the backside. Reluctantly she went out to the kitchen to make some coffee.

He came out of the bedroom dressed in Levi's and a sport shirt and ready to go. He could smell the freshly brewed coffee as Barb filled two of their familiar cream-colored mugs. She sat down at the little round table and looked out at the gray sky. Steve sat down and took a sip. It was very hot. "I really gotta go," he said slowly and softly. "Can't miss the bus."

"I know," said Barbara. "I'll see you tonight."

Steve took another sip from his mug, then stood up and stepped back from the table. Barbara did not look his way, but just kept looking outside.

Steve walked toward the door and he heard her chair move. She got up and ran over to him and grabbed him in a powerful embrace. "I know there's hope, but where's the possibility?"

Steve could see the tears starting to form in her eyes. "Hey, take it easy, my pretty girl. I'll be home tonight, and we'll figure out what the next step is then." They embraced for what seemed like both a long time and not enough time, then kissed. Steve held her hand as he turned and started toward the door. They both took a deep breath, let go, and Steve rushed out, letting the screen door slam shut as he left. He had to run the last fifty yards to catch the bus, but he made it just in time.

He had no choice but to take the physical. Now he was on the bus heading downtown on a grayish-brown, smog-filled day. Taking a deep breath of that downtown Los Angeles air was like breathing soot. *When we get out of school, we're moving somewhere without smog*, he thought. The bus ride took forty-five minutes with one transfer. But that was no big deal. It was better to leave the Mustang with Barbara so she could get to and from her work at the rest home. Neither one of them was happy about this turn of events, and even with her super-positive attitude, she was stumped. It looked like there was no way out. But there was a flip side. Both Barbara and Steve believed they were patriotic, and this was their call to duty—a call to be taken seriously. While others burned their draft cards and moved to Canada, they felt their country was calling and the cause must be just. Lots of their friends had gone into the military before them, some right out of high school. Now it was Steve's turn.

After Steve got off the bus in downtown LA, he only had to walk one block to the address on his instruction card. He entered an old seven-story brick building that was almost hidden among the taller downtown skyscrapers. He was met by the backs of thirty or so other young men—some might say boys—who were queued up in front of him. They were probably between eighteen and twenty four, probably from most walks of life, probably not from wealthy families. As others arrived, the line grew behind him.

The building was like an old multi-story warehouse that had been pressed into service to handle the large volume of recruits coming through the system. Temporary partitions were everywhere around the large rooms. When he got to the desk, the three NCOs seated there were just taking names and directing traffic. Steve gave them his card and his name, and a frumpy female sergeant in front of him looked up his name in a card file and pointed to the floor. "See that yellow line? Take these forms, follow that line up those stairs, and do what the next person tells you. Got it?"

He nodded and walked off down the yellow line—which, he thought ironically, might just as well have been a yellow brick road taking him in a new direction in life. But all he really wanted was to click his heels and be magically transported back home to Barb.

The whole day was like that. Follow the yellow line. Follow the blue line. Go up two flights of stairs to take a long written test. Then he was directed to a large room on the fourth floor with desks like a classroom. He'd never seen so much paperwork. There were forms to give your life history, health history; triplicate forms to say you understood the other forms, and on and on.

Then it was on to the line to be weighed and poked—and finally, examined by a doctor. Standing in line dressed only in underwear left you feeling vulnerable. Steve was a little embarrassed that he was not as buff as some of the guys, but he was proud that at least he was not chubby, like some of the others.

Around noon they handed out lunch vouchers and were told to take thirty minutes and go find something to eat. There were several restaurants in the area that accepted the vouchers. Steve had a ham sandwich and a Coca Cola at a deli. Then it was back to his place in line for more of the same. He endured a final question-and-answer session back on the first floor with a well-spoken sergeant.

That was it, and he was done by just after four in the afternoon. He found his way back out to the street, and after a ten minute wait, hopped on the bus for the ride home.

When he walked in the door of the little apartment, he caught the wonderful smell of Barbara's special meat loaf, seasoned with her secret spices. When he looked around, he saw that she was waiting in the kitchen. He knew there'd be a lot of questions. As she checked the oven, she said in a resigned voice, "Well, I assume you passed."

He came over behind her, reached around her waist, and gave her a tender hug. He kissed her gently on the back of the neck and said, "Don't know for sure, but I think so. They culled a few guys out as we went through the exams. I think those were the ones that didn't make it."

He went to the sink, turned on the tap, stuck his head under it, and took a drink. "Use a glass," she said with mock severity.

"Yes, Mother," he replied.

"So when will you know for sure?"

He walked over to the breakfast nook, wiping his mouth off on his sleeve as he went, and looked out the window. "They said we could get a letter in a few days telling us what we do next," he said. "I only see one other option." He looked out the window at the red sky and setting sun, then muttered, "Red sky at night, sailors delight."

"What did you say?" said Barbara.

"Oh, it's an old sailor's expression about the weather. You can tell by the color of the sky what kind of weather you're going to have. 'Red sky in the morning, sailors take warning. Red sky at night, sailors delight.' I'm just looking at this beautiful sunset and wondering if it's a sign that everything is going to work out." He turned back around and looked at his wife. *I'm so lucky*, he thought, *Beautiful and smart, and for some reason she loves me.* He pulled out the chair at the table and sat down.

Barbara came over and sat down in his lap. He instinctively put his arm around her slender waist and gave her another gentle hug. "Of course it's going to work out," she said. "I don't know how, and neither do you, but you and me—we're going to have a great life. Got it, Buster?" And then she smiled, turned, and looked out the window. "If smog can do that to a sky, then a few gray clouds in our life are just going to make a better sunset. Now . . . tell me the options."

Steve looked at her, meeting her stunning blue eyes. He took a deep breath and replied: "Well, there are only two that I can see. One, I accept getting drafted and hope for the best. Or"—he hesitated a moment—"two, I can enlist." He didn't have long to wait for her reaction.

A puzzled look came over Barb's face. "Enlist? What does that do for you?"

"Well, for one thing, it gives me more options. For one thing, I can choose army, navy, air force, or marines."

"Okay, you wanted to try for flight school. Why not go for the air force?

"Aye—there's the rub," he said. trying for a little Hamlet.

"What do you mean?"

"Well, that's what I'd like to do more than anything, but to get flight school in the air force, I'd need a four-year degree. It's the same thing with the navy and marines."

Barb didn't understand where this was going. "Well, okay. So what field do you shoot for?"

He looked down, avoiding her questioning eyes. "I still want to go for aviation." He took a deep breath and looked up. "I talked to a recruiter a couple of days ago, and he said that the army has no college requirements for flight school. You just have to pass some tests."

"Good, then go army. Does that mean you would be flying helicopters?"

"Well, maybe, if I could get a flight school slot, but the recruiter guy says I can't. He says I have to go through an officers' program first. There are two kinds. One is called a "Warrant Officer," and I'm not quite sure what that is, and the other is Officer Candidate School—OCS." He let out a short sigh. "He says there are no slots for those either."

Barbara cocked her head to one side. "What is this, a good news-bad news joke?"

"Yeah, kinda like that. Just stick with me for a minute on this, okay?"

"So cut to the chase," she said with a slight edge to her voice.

"Okay. The recruiter did say that he could get me a slot as a helicopter mechanic and crew chief on a helicopter, so I could go to school as a maintenance tech, and he said that sometimes they get promoted to pilot."

"A recruiter told you this?" she asked with a hint of sarcasm.

"Said he would put it in writing. Anyhow, I think it's my best shot."

Barbara got up off of his lap and sat down in the chair facing him. "And you would be leaving when?"

"In about six weeks—if you agree. Probably eight weeks if I wait for the final draft notice."

"Not much time either way," she said, the resignation in her voice evident. "I'll keep the meatloaf warm. Let's continue this conversation in there." She smiled and winked, then nodded toward the bedroom. Steve took her hands in his, stood up, and pulled her to him. Their eyes were locked on together as he brought her mouth to his. They closed their eyes and kissed like only two people in love can kiss. Time and space vanished. She felt his hand slide down her back to her waist, then felt the gentle squeeze on her shapely butt. Standing, pressed up against him, she felt his manhood rising. She took the hand that was holding her and stepped back, drawing him with her as she moved toward the bedroom. With her other hand she began to unbutton his shirt. She fell back on the bed and, following her motion, he gently laid on top of her, kissing her neck, then embracing and kissing her hard on the lips again.

* * *

After they finished Barb's amazing meatloaf and a couple glasses of inexpensive red wine, they had a repeat performance in the bedroom. They finally fell asleep around midnight, still in an embrace, Barbara's head on Steve's chest.

* * *

That seemed like ages ago. Steve had taken the recruiters advice and enlisted in the army. He'd gotten orders to basic training at Fort Polk, Louisiana. They were apart for eight long weeks. Then, after a short leave, he was sent to Fort Ord, California for another eight weeks of training, and in California they occasionally got to see each other on the weekends. After that, he was sent to Fort Benning, Georgia, for OCS. It seemed that the army discovered he was eligible for officers training, thanks to the tests he'd taken. It was more of the "good news, bad news." The good news was that he was on his way to becoming an officer. The bad news was that it was infantry training, so he'd graduate as an, infantry second lieutenant—and, according to statistics, his life expectancy as a platoon leader in the field would not be measured in years, or even months, but in days. In one sense, what they'd hoped for was coming true, but there were still a lot of "ifs." The biggest "if" was if he would get assigned to flight school. That would meet his second goal.

OCS was tough though. Nearly half of his class had washed out. But somehow, after nearly six months, it was apparent that he was going to make it. Steve felt that he was leading a charmed life. About three weeks before he graduated from OCS, he received word that he'd been accepted to the US Army Flight School program. And even better news—it was not for helicopters, but for fixed-wing aircraft. Less than two percent of flight school candidates got fixed wing. The angel on his shoulder had come through again.

During the six months of OCS, Barbara stayed in California. It just was not cost-effective or practical for her to go all the way to Georgia in hopes that Steve would have a couple of days off now and then to spend with her. Their separation was just about killing them, though. Steve faithfully wrote love letters to his wife several times a week. Barbara wrote back two or three times a day. She sent pictures of herself at work, with her friends, and of the sunsets.

When Steve graduated from OCS, he was assigned to a basic training company at Fort Benning as a training officer while awaiting orders for flight school. He had two weeks leave saved up, and nothing was going to keep them apart again. He'd prepped Barbara for the possibility of what might happen, and she'd already given notice on their apartment. When he got back to LA, they packed up the few things they had accumulated—mainly dishes, linens, and clothes—and packed them in the car. Steve had a trailer hitch put on the Mustang, and they rented a U-Haul for the few larger things they had, and they were on their way to Georgia. On the side of the trailer it said, "Adventure in Moving." It was a prophecy of what was to come—not just for this trip, but for a lifetime.

* * *

And now here she was, living in Dothan, Alabama, about fifteen miles from the front gate of Fort Rucker, the home of US Army Aviation. Her husband had graduated fixed-wing flight school about six months earlier. It was a little over four months ago that his orders put him on an Air Force C-121 transport to Travis Air Force Base in California, a little ways from Sacramento. From there he caught a contract flight with Flying Tigers, a Boeing 707 that took him to Saigon via Hawaii, Wake Island, and the Philippines.

It was just another small apartment, but it was where they'd lived the whole time Steve was going through flight school. He'd been promoted to first lieutenant shortly after arriving at Fort Rucker. While there, he was not only receiving his base pay, but also flight pay and TDY (temporary duty) pay—and combined with her income from the nursing position she'd found at the Dothan Hospital, they made a pretty good living.

They'd traded in the Mustang on an almost new 1968 Corvette convertible, blue with a white top. Since they had no kids yet, it worked out fine. During flight school days, Steve rode onto the base with his student pilot stick-mate, Mike, who lived a couple of doors down in the apartment complex. Mike was married to a cute redhead from Savannah. Her friends all just called her "Copper," or "Cop," for short. On days off they spent time together barbecuing and watching *The Prisoner* on the little black and white TV at Mike and Copper's house.

Since they knew that the next assignment after flight school would probably be Vietnam, Steve and Barbara also spent a lot of time making love and holding hands, and just looking in each other's eyes. The future was not something that they talked a lot about. Their conversations were more just about the next couple of years.

Copper and Barbara became stalwarts in the Student Pilot Officers Wives Club. There was no official sanction. It was just something the two of them came up with. When they started it, they knew that in the not-to-distant future both their husbands and a lot of others would be heading out to distant places, and it would be good to have a support network. They met once a week, and together began preparation for the days to come.

And since its beginning almost a year ago, the club still met. Some of the wives had moved back home with parents or friends while their husbands were gone, so the group was a little smaller. A couple of add-ons from other flight school classes had joined the group. They helped each other out with needs like babysitting and taking care of each other when one was sick. Most of all, they were there as a shoulder to cry on as news came in from the war zone.

Sure enough, two weeks before graduation, the orders came down. A couple of the guys in Steve's class had been assigned to advanced aircraft training, but most had overseas assignments. Most of the overseas assignments were to Vietnam. Steve was in that lucky group. It was late October when he got on the transport plane that would send him on his journey to the other side of the world.

Barbara was hoping that all of their lovemaking just before Steve left would leave them with a little present in about eight or nine months, but it was not to be. Several of the other girls were now many months pregnant. She confided in Copper about her concerns, and they talked it over. She decided to have a doctor friend at the hospital run a simple test to see if there was a physical reason she did not conceive. The news had come back, and her heart sank as she learned. It wasn't going to happen. She didn't want to write Steve about it, but she knew she had to. He had the right to know.

As always, Steve's reply was filled with love and understanding, telling her that there would be a way and they would figure it out together. He told her that it was a few months until she would be able to meet him on R&R in Hawaii. She was anxious to hold him and cry with him, and hear his comforting words from his lips and not just read them in some letter. She was already starting to pack for the trip. She just prayed to God she could hold it together for a couple more months.

Chapter 4

Sister Ellen awoke with a start. After twenty years, you'd think a person would get used to the sound of automatic gunfire. It was something the sisters lived with. Every couple of days you would hear it. Sometimes close, sometimes off in the distance. Sometimes it was just day after day. Then there was the sound of the helicopters. Phu Loi, the US Army base, was only about thirty klicks to the south, and when the departing helicopters flew north, they came right over the convent. The last couple of months it has been fairly quiet, and she was starting to get used to the quiet. She felt her prayers could be heard better in the quiet.

She sat up in her bed, turned, and eased out from under the sheets. She slid the mosquito netting to one side, and as her feet found the hard wooden floor, she felt around and found the simple brown thong sandals that were beside her bed. She slipped them on. Quietly, she went out into the darkened hallway and walked to the window at the end. She looked through the glass protected with black painted steel bars on the outside and into the darkness beyond and listened. Off in the distance she saw the crimson red arc of tracers fired one way, and then back the other way as two enemies forces attempted to destroy each other. It was a foreboding thought, especially for a nun, someone who had devoted herself to preserving life—or at least preparing lives for an unknown and uncertain eternity.

But that wasn't her main concern now. The children were tucked in their beds awaiting the morning, and those precious charges were her priority. This was her service to God. She prayed daily that the war would end, but the most she could allow herself to hope for was that the fighting would at least pass by their little island of protection and leave them alone, untouched.

The little convent and its buildings and grounds were not much to look at. If you looked more closely, you could see the remnants of a proud past. When the French had been the dominant foreign force in the territory, the area surrounding the convent was a rubber plantation. The stucco-covered building was the main plantation home and headquarters. It had housed the overseer. Wonderful and elaborate dinners and elegant parties were held in its ballroom. Hunting parties of wealthy European businessmen were entertained between forays into the jungle to hunt tiger and bull elephant. Even Theodore Roosevelt had once spent a short time in the comfort of these walls when he stopped over on his way to the central highland area of Da Lat.

Most of its classical beauty was now a thing of the past. The basic structure was still intact, but when the French pulled out, everything of value was removed. Other than the size of the main building, the only things that hinted of its bygone grandeur that remained untouched were the curving staircase and the carved wooden banister leading from the once-majestic entry to the second floor living quarters. There was also the large fireplace at the end of the great hall that was made of river rock. It was large enough for a small boy to stand up inside of it.

How the nuns had come to take possession of the old plantation was a story in itself. But for them, it was an answer to prayer. They needed a place to provide a refuge for their children, a place away from the war. And by some miracle, this was the place.

Where once row upon row of tall, lush rubber trees and jungle had surrounded the plantation buildings, now only bare ground and leafless trees could be seen, and that lifelessness seemed to extend for miles. They had their small gardens for growing what food they could. But the dense foliage was gone. Such was the horrible effect of Agent Orange. The faded white stucco buildings, with peeling white paint, their edges covered in mildew, looked out of place standing starkly naked in a man-made desert. The whole effect was one of deserted loneliness.

Sister Ellen felt a hand touch her shoulder, which startled her. She jumped, letting out a short cry, and turned to hear Sister Louise saying "Shh—it's only me." She breathed a sigh of relief, patted herself on her chest, then reached out and took Louise by the hand and pulled her gently toward her. They wrapped their arms together and stood side-by-side and watched the battle and its drama as it unfolded, as they could see it through the partially opened window.

"They're a long ways off, Ellen," whispered Louise in French. "Lets check on the children and get back to bed."

Ellen nodded, and they turned and walked slowly back down the upstairs hall arm in arm. In the big room at the end of the upstairs hall, twenty-three children slept. They were mostly three to seven years old, although there were a couple of older ones. Most slept on the floor on little woven pads. There were a couple of cots too. Sister Evon slept peacefully in her four-poster bed against the wall, with one of the youngest beside her. The four-poster was covered with the ubiquitous mosquito netting, a necessity in this climate.

"See, everything's fine," whispered Louise. "Go back to sleep."

"How much longer, Sister Louise? How much longer will it go on? I don't know if I can take much more. I don't know how much more the children can take. Will it ever end?"

In the early hours just before morning, with stars still shining in the sky, Sister Louise could see the emotion on Sister Ellen's face, the tears in her eyes. She knew that Ellen thought of each of the children as her own. She gave them all the love any mother could give a child. Yet there was nothing she could do to protect them from a seemingly inevitable fate. But if the war was over, she felt that then there could be a time for healing.

"Pray that this dawn will bring us a better day," said Sister Louise in a quiet, reassuring voice. "It's all we can do. Now go to bed, please. I'll see you when daylight is fully come."

At that moment, a flight of six Hueys flew over the convent, leaving a fading trail of chop-chop-chop sounds as they flew northward. They held each other until they couldn't hear them anymore. Then without any further words, they gave each other a final hug and went back to their beds.

As Sister Ellen drifted off, she remembered her youth in her small village in northern France. Her parents had passed away before she was twelve. First her Mom went, and then a year later her Dad. She'd been sent to live at a convent run by Carmelite nuns in the countryside not far from her village. It was there that she learned the power of prayer and the joy of caring for others. She never dreamed that she would be called to serve in a place so far away. But here she was. She smiled as she thought about her children, and then sleep overtook her.

She awoke a few hours later, surprised to find that it was fully light outside. She heard a Jeep horn honking. Quickly she got up, put on her habit, and looked out the window. A smile came to her face as she saw the Jeep and driver. She could see that the muddy Jeep was loaded with boxes, and she could see the stupid-looking grin and the friendly wave that came from the army guy they just knew as Pop. She looked beyond his out-of-place brown ten-gallon cowboy hat and saw the angel that had just driven into her courtyard.

Chapter 5

It was just before eleven o'clock at night. The flight-line was mostly dark, and there were a multitude of stars shining down from above. Captains Steve Armanski and Terry Downey were standing beside a large single-engine aircraft.

"It's a great old airplane," said Ski, "a little slow and lumbering, but a great old plane. There aren't many single-engine planes that can carry the load this old Beaver can." They got on board, Downey in the right seat and Armanski in the left. Shortly after that, they were airborne and on their way to Saigon.

To Terry, it felt good to have a helmet with earphones and a boom microphone that was always right there next to his lips. The intercom and the radio transmissions came through so clear. The civilian aircraft he'd been used to flying usually had a hand-held mike and an overhead speaker that competed with the loud drone of the engine. The helmet was also intended to protect against head injuries in case of a crash, but the coziness of the built-in headphones and mike were certainly a welcome bonus.

This was Terry's first flight in a Beaver, and his first night mission flying mortar watch over Saigon. Steve Armanski—Ski—was giving him the full briefing on the aircraft. Terry had drawn the copilot slot to fly with him for the next two weeks. It would be four hours over Saigon from 11 p.m. to 3 a.m. every night. The part that was physically draining was, he still had to fly his regular Bird Dog missions during the day. But he'd volunteered. It was a chance to fly a different airplane, and maybe get qualified in it. He was always one to do a little more than average, and he just felt he was young enough and strong enough—

and motivated enough—to pull it off. Little did he know that this airplane would hold a key place in his future activities.

In the Beaver, the pilots sat side by side. Normally there were seats for at least seven more behind the pilots, but on this mission all the seats had been removed or folded up, and a large, octagonal-shaped tear gas canister, filled with about 500 individual gas grenades, had been placed in the center of the floor. It was about three feet long and about eighteen inches in diameter. That was the reason for the copilot. The canister was so large, awkward, and heavy that there was no way to get the canister out of the plane without someone physically opening the side cargo door and pushing it out. That was the copilot's job, and since it weighed about 300 pounds, even that was a job that required two people. Because the gas canister was designed to explode when it came close to the ground, so as to spread out the smaller grenades and cover a large area, they made the crew carry gas masks, in case there was an accident and it went off inside the plane.

As they flew, Ski recited what he knew about the Beaver. "The Pratt & Whitney R-985 radial engine is one of the best ever built. These planes have been known to have up to three out of the nine cylinders shot out and still have enough power to limp a hundred miles back to home base. I wouldn't want to have to try it though." He went on as if he were the all-time Beaver expert. He was certainly a good pilot, but he hadn't been flying them that long himself.

Terry guessed the thing that made him kind of special was that he had gotten his Beaver training before arriving in-country, and there was only one Beaver in the company. Only he and the CO were qualified to fly it. It made him a one-of-a-kind pilot in their little group of forty or so pilots.

After a couple of the night flights, Armanski quit talking about the airplane so much and talked about other things that interested him. He told Terry about the little orphanage just north of Phu Loi, and how he and Pop Danforth would go up there and take supplies to the kids. Ski had a soft spot in his heart for kids. He was always trying to do something special for them. He felt it was his special mission. They talked a lot on those flights because there wasn't much else to do. Sometimes they tuned in the ADF radio to AFVN and listened to music. It was the only radio station in English, so it was the only one they ever listened to. Not much choice. You just got whatever they decided to play.

For several weeks they flew that midnight mortar watch. Their assigned area to patrol was called Charlie Corridor. Not that there were more VC there than other places—there was an Alpha and Bravo corridor too. Together, three aircraft on watch could fly a triangle of cover over the outskirts of Saigon and look for mortar flashes or rocket launches. If they saw them soon enough, they could call in and warn the troops on the ground that they were under attack, and they could take cover. Thirty seconds of warning could mean the difference between life and death. Then they could ask permission to drop the gas canister on the area where they saw the flashes or rocket trails. But that was a huge hassle. They had no power to do it on their own—even though they saw exactly where the target was and knew that the fire was directed at their own troops. They had to call headquarters for clearance. Then HQ had to call the Vietnamese commander and ask permission, and he had to call the RVN commander, who called the province chief to ask permission, and by the time they had any kind of answer, it was too late to do any good. The couple of times they'd asked for clearance they'd waited over an hour, and the answer was "negative—do not drop." It was the beauty of politics. It didn't matter where in the world a person went—there was always politics.

Sometimes Terry wondered why they were up there. *Just for the warning,* he thought, *so our guys have time to duck under cover before another barrage.*

Recon Airplane Company: III Corps, Vietnam

One night a civilian rock band came to play for the troops stationed at Phu Loi—a so-so tour group from the States that had come over to entertain the homesick soldiers. Their show would end at 2200 hours, and for some reason Ski got it in his head to invite the lead singer and her husband, the lead guitarist, to join them on the nights mission and fly mortar watch.

The two musicians were excited about getting to see more of the war and flying in a military aircraft. It was against regulations for civilians to be in military aircraft without clearance—*but what the heck*, thought Ski. *If we get caught, what can they do to us—send us to Vietnam?* Ski talked Pulaski, the crew chief, into removing the gas canister and putting in two passenger seats. "Who cares?" he'd said to Terry. "They've never used that stupid gas canister anyway."

He got two extra sets of Nomex flight suits and delivered them and two flight helmets to the room where the band members were staying. At about 2245 hours, Ski and Terry went by the room. The two musicians came out looking a lot like any other army pilots, and they went down to the flight line.

"Keep the pony tail tucked in," Ski cautioned the girl. "We could get in big trouble for this. And don't stand up so straight. It may be dark out here, but there are a couple of things about you that might distinguish you from a regular pilot. And believe me—I mean that in a good way. Once we're in the plane you can relax and enjoy the ride."

The singer laughed. "Is that all that men think about?"

Ski looked at Terry and they said in unison, "Pretty much!" They went on toward the flight line.

Ski had a great heart, but bad timing. The crew chief was at the plane when they arrived. Ski had told him not to bother to meet them and to go to bed early. But now, since he'd seen the illegal passengers, they had to swear him to secrecy. He was willing to swear *if* he could also go along on the flight. Ski figured it had to do with only being around guys for so long time.

Being near a girl now was making him act strange. The crew chief had never wanted to fly with them before—he'd always said that flying made him sick.

The Beaver could be started a couple of ways, but the primary way was with the electric inertial starter. Typically in a car, you just turned the key and the direct drive went straight to the crankshaft and turned it over. This old style radial engine had something different. After priming the engine, then setting the throttle, the pilot held up the starter switch until he could hear the heavy inertial flywheel speeding faster and faster, and when it reached its apex he would throw a second switch, which would engage the crankshaft to the flywheel and start the crankshaft turning, and subsequently the pistons pumping and the propeller spinning. Then he had to wait for it to turn over twice by watching the propeller blades go by, and with his other hand he would engage the magnetos. All this while holding on to the wobble pump that supplied initial fuel pressure until the engine sputtered to life, and then the engine-driven fuel pump would take over. It looked a bit like a choreographed ballet in the cramped cockpit. An experienced pilot could make it look easy. Once the engine began running smoothly, things got simple again. Now the pilot just had to concern himself with the throttle, and taxiing this very large, single-engine, tail-dragger.

On smaller aircraft, in an emergency, if the starter failed to operate, or if the battery was dead, a pilot could set the switches and crank the propeller over by hand. This was called "propping." But the reason the Beaver had such a complicated starting system was because it was originally designed as a back woods bush plane, and due to the size of the engine and how far the prop was off the ground, it was nearly impossible for a person to start it by propping. So someone came up with the inertial starter.

You could start a Beaver with a hand crank, but this took two people. On the left side of the airplane was a hole. The crank was inserted into the hole until it engaged the inertial starter mechanism. The pilot would go through his normal prestart routine, and then the second person would balance himself precariously on the step next to the cowl and the wing strut. He would grab the crank handle with both hands and start turning it. It took several seconds just to get it to start moving, but once it started moving the crank could be turned faster and faster as the momentum developed. When the pilot heard the special sound that told him it was up to speed, he would engage the clutch to the motor by pulling a cable connected to a handle, and the prop would start to spin. The rest of the procedure was the same.

It was a selling point to the army because it allowed the aircraft to be started without electrical power. If the battery or electrical system failed, the aircraft could still be started and flown. No other regular electrical power was needed. Even the flaps were hydraulic and operated by a hand pump. So this legendary bush plane was also an excellent army aircraft. It was one of a series of aircraft made by de Havilland of Canada that were built to withstand the rugged wilderness of the northern most regions of the American continent.

After Ski got it started, they taxied out of the revetment area and headed for the runway. For them it was routine, but they looked at one another and smiled, because they could both sense the excitement in the seats behind them. "God, please grant us a boring night," Terry breathed into his mike as Ski applied the throttle for takeoff.

They were in the air and on the way to Charlie Corridor before 2300 hours. Terry tuned the radio to Company Frequency and told the Bird Dog pilot currently on duty there that they were on their way and that he was cleared to head for home. It only took about fifteen minutes to get to the northern end of Charlie Corridor, and about five minutes after they arrived, Terry heard the Bird Dog call for landing instructions at Phu Loi. This was going to be a nice night. The air was calm, the engine was running extra smoothly, and there was a faint scent of perfume coming up from the back seat. Terry almost felt like he was back home with a girlfriend, flying in his dad's old Cherokee 160 up the San Joaquin valley on the way to the Nut Tree for dinner.

Ski set the throttle and prop controls to low cruise, and with his right hand reached down to the flap handle and pumped in about three degrees of flaps. That not only reduced the noise level, it also raised the tail to put the airplane in a more nose level position. This made it easier to see beyond the engine cowling, which otherwise blocked the view out of the windshield. Terry started to relax.

They flew the corridor for about an hour, first one way and then the other. They pointed out the various sights to their passengers. The singer chick stuck her head between the two pilots as they talked about the various lights on the ground. It was so nice—the smell, the soft voice.

And then it happened. Terry saw them first, the little flashes on the ground, like flashbulbs going off. There was about six of them, and they were way out in the blackness of the area known as the Run Sat Special Zone, just southeast of Saigon. "Ski," Terry shouted into his mike, "dead ahead, just next to the point at the end of the corridor. Mortars!"

Ski pushed the nose over as Terry switched the radio to transmit. "Charlie Control, Charlie Control, this is Aloft Four-Two. You have incoming—repeat, you have incoming."

"Damn," said Ski, "not tonight!"

By now the passengers had undone their seat belts and were leaning forward to look over the pilots' shoulders to see all the action. "Sit down," Terry said, "and buckle up."

The radio squelched and the voice of Charlie Control said in a calm voice, "Can you give me the coordinates of the activity?"

"Roger," Terry answered. "Just give me a minute." He picked up his map and marked the location. "Four-six-five-eight, five-five-seven-six—repeat: four-six-five-eight, five-five-seven-six," he reported crisply. "Do you copy?"

Control verified the numbers then asked the fateful question. "Would you like permission to drop gas?"

Terry looked over at Ski and said, "Gas, hell. I think I just shit my pants." They both laughed nervously.

Ski keyed the intercom. "Stall 'em. What do we do now?" He was excited and nervous. A couple months with nothing happening, and now a major mortar attack—and their magic weapon was on the ground in the Beavers' revetment back at Phu Loi.

"Hey, don't ask me," Terry answered. "You're the senior pilot on this deal, and this rock band trip was your idea, remember?" He keyed his transmitter. "Charlie Control? Can you get us clearance to drop gas?" he asked, trying to sound like he meant it.

"Stand by, Aloft," came the reply. "We're working on it."

Terry looked over at Ski, who still looked irritated and nervous. "Relax, Ski—we've never gotten the stupid clearance before. What makes you think well get it now?"

"Just look out there. That's the most mortar activity I've ever seen. Tonight," he said disgustedly, "tonight we'll get the clearance."

"So," Terry said, "what if we do. Remember Saunders? He got clearance to drop, and he put it right on target—at least that's what he said."

"Yeah," Ski said with a chuckle, "and it never went off."

"It probably did, but it was just twenty feet under that silt and mud down there in the delta. At any rate, they never found it."

"We'll just tell 'em we dropped it then," said Ski.

"Your baby," Terry replied. "You're the aircraft commander."

"Thanks for reminding me . . . again," replied an annoyed Ski.

Their guests didn't have jacks to plug in their headsets, so all they could hear was the steady drone of the engine. The crew chief was a different matter. When he saw the commotion in the cockpit and felt the aircraft nose over, the engine throttle up, and the flaps go back to full up, he knew something was going on and went to the rear seat, where there was a headset jack. He plugged in and heard most of the conversation, then keyed his mike and said, "Guess I have some dirt for the CO, don't I."

"Okay, Pulaski, how long you been listening in?" said Ski.

"Long enough," said the crew chief.

"I guess you're going to tell him how you took the gas off the airplane and why you came along for a ride, huh?" Terry said, putting in his two-cents worth.

"But I'm not the aircraft commander," Pulaski said with a chuckle. "I was just following orders."

"No you weren't," said Ski. "You volunteered. You actually disobeyed orders when you showed up at the revetment when I told you to get lost. You're in this as deep as we are."

There was a moment of silence, then Pulaski said, "Touché. I guess we can just hope we don't get caught."

Twenty minutes had gone by after the initial attack, and they still hadn't received clearance to drop the gas. The mortar attack had only lasted for three or four minutes, but that was long enough for the command at Tan Son Nhut Air Base in Saigon to launch three F-4 fighters, which had begun to strafe the area.

The radio crackled to life. "Aloft, we have permission for you to drop. Give it your best. Copy?"

"Roger," Terry answered, "clearance to drop." Armanski looked at Terry and rolled his eyes. Terry looked back and chuckled. "Military efficiency," he said.

It was about fifteen minutes after midnight. The area where the mortars had been fired from was now quiet and dark. Earlier they'd heard the report that some of the mortar rounds had landed on Tan Son Nhut's perimeter, but no one was hurt. Their advance warning had alerted the ground forces to sound sirens, and two perimeter guards were able to duck for cover before the shells landed just a few feet from their outpost. At least something had worked out right.

Recon Airplane Company: III Corps, Vietnam

"Well, the transponder is on, so they have us on radar," Terry said. "Let's make it look good." They flew over the launch site and slowed the plane for a couple minutes, just like they would do if this was for real. Then they called Charlie Control. "Gas away," Terry reported, and was greeted with a simple "Roger."

They still had over two hours to go before returning home. Ski trimmed the Beaver back to slow flight again and headed back toward Charlie Corridor. He put down some flaps, then said, "You take it, Terry. All this excitement has worn me out. I'm going to get a little sleep." He settled back in his seat and put his head against the side of the plane by the window. He'd barely started to relax when he suddenly sat straight up. "Shit!" he said in a loud voice over the intercom. "They think we launched our gas. How are we going to explain the canister we still have?"

His mind began to spin. Calm down, he thought. *You'll figure something out. You're dealing with the military and their legendary efficiency, for God's sake.* He didn't even try to sleep after that. Two hours later they turned the airplane back toward home base.

As they flew over the base preparing their approach, they noticed that there seemed to be too many lights around the company flight line. It was normally pretty black this time of night—four in the morning. What was going on? They tried to figure out a plan to explain it, but it was no use. They just knew they were on their way to a court-martial. They could both feel it. Maybe they could come up with a plan to minimize it. Surely there was something they could do.

Ski landed long, farther down the runway than usual, and continued his landing roll to the end, the farthest point from the company area. Then he turned around and onto the taxiway, nose pointed back to the Beaver's parking place. He stopped. "Pulaski!" he shouted over the intercom. "Walk these two home. Try not to be seen. Terry and I will try to bluff our way out of the rest."

"Uh, what's this 'Terry and I' shit. You're the aircraft commander," Terry said, laughing out loud.

"Shut up," said Ski. "I don't need another reminder."

"Good luck, Sir," came a delayed, hushed reply from Pulaski. He took off his helmet and tossed it up on the back seat. Then he opened the side door, jumped out, and helped the would-be rock stars out into the blackness alongside the airstrip. The sound of the big radial engine, with the pop and sputter of its idle, was all they could hear. Pulaski walked toward the company area alongside the taxiway and guided the couple into the compound, being careful to avoid prying eyes until they got within sight of the guest quarters and then told them that they'd have to walk alone from there.

In the meantime, the two Beaver pilots advanced the throttle and started to taxi once again, slowly now as they discussed their options. It was about 5,000 feet back to the revetment area, nearly the entire length of the runway, and they were both starting to sweat. It was extra warm that night—or at least it seemed that way. They both opened their cockpit doors and used their knees to prop them open so the air could flow in as they taxied. The last traces of the perfume wafted up to the cockpit and then just slowly faded away. Even at this point, Terry felt it almost seemed worth it.

They taxied into the designated parking spot in the forward revetment, but to their surprise no one was there. They were expecting the CO and armed guards to escort them to the detention center. What they saw besides the extra lights were people bustling about by the maintenance shed. But no one seemed to care about them. They parked the Beaver, shut down the engine, and got out. On the ground next to the wall was the gas canister, right where they'd left it. They took out the passenger seats and put them in the storage shed. Then they picked up the canister and, with a great deal of effort, they lifted it back into the Beaver's cargo area. They closed the side cargo door, tied the aircraft down, and filled out their logbook. As they headed back to the sandbagged building they called their hooch, they made a pact to deal with the "extra" gas canister in the morning—if, by some magic, they weren't standing at attention in front of the CO.

Pulaski, meanwhile, had finished his mission, checked out the situation, and had come back to meet the pilots. He was waiting for them just outside the sandbag wall. "They're back in their hooch all safe and sound," he said. "They said they wouldn't breathe a word and they have no idea what really happened up there. They said to say thanks."

Ski said to him, "Do you have any idea what's going on here tonight? It's after four in the morning. What's with all the lights?"

Pulaski looked down at the ground. "Lt. Lambert," he said solemnly. "He crashed around 2400 tonight. Just off the end of the runway. They still don't know why. Guess they'll have to look it over when it gets light. He just made it inside the perimeter fence. They're not going to try to take his body out until morning, when it's light enough to do a proper investigation."

They didn't go back to their hooches that night. The club at the end of the Officers' Quarters was full, but the mood was somber. Some were talking about the airplane that had crashed—old seven-five-seven, one of the best flying planes they had. Someone said something about how come it was always the nice guys that bought it. Most were just sitting around the tables in quiet reflection, having a drink. He was here with them yesterday. Tom was just about the nicest guy in the company. He was a handsome young man, a good Catholic boy. Everybody liked him a lot. He'd only been in country for six weeks.

They'd just left the gas canister on the Beaver and didn't requisition another one. They wouldn't talk about that night unless they were off alone somewhere. The army, as was typical, never figured it out. It really didn't matter. The next night they flew Charlie Corridor again. The gas canister was safely aboard, but they never got clearance to use it again.

About two weeks later, Terry quit flying the Beaver with Armanski. He was building up too many hours in his daytime missions and had to cut back to stay within regulations. He flew Charlie Corridor again though, on Christmas Eve, in his trusty Bird Dog with another stupid 300-pound gas canister shackled to a hard point on the right wing. It made the airplane so heavy he could barely get off the ground. He told Armanski that it felt as though he had Capt. Mike Ballard in the back seat. The old San Francisco cop, nicknamed Capt. Bastard, who must have weighed 300 pounds. No one could figure out how he even got into the airplane. But that's another story.

Chapter 6

Armanski was sitting in Terry's room across from him on the bunk. It was semi-dark and sort of cool because the air conditioner was working that day. They were talking about some guys stationed in the middle of nowhere, and as always, Ski wanted to make them feel better. Terry suggested that they see a chaplain.

"Come on, Terry," said Ski. "Those guys deserve a little Christmas cheer too."

"I dunno," said Terry as though he really didn't care. "What's so special about them?"

"Well, for one thing, they're all alone on that mound out there in the middle of nowhere, and all they get to do is talk to people on the radio," said Ski. "It's boring as hell, but every now and then they get to look Charlie in the eye. Tell you what. My mission today takes me right over 'em. You're off today, so why not come along and see what I mean?"

"You mean as if I need another day of flying," Terry said with a sigh. "And you and I really don't have the best luck on 'special missions,' if I remember right."

"You can ride in the back seat," Ski said enthusiastically. "Sleep back there anytime you want."

"Now you want me to risk my life with you at the controls?" said Terry, only half joking. "Didn't I get enough of that in the Beaver? And then you even think I could sleep? Ah, what the hell." Doing something—anything—out of the ordinary sounded better to Terry than just sitting around all day. "It's boring here anyway."

Lt. Armanski was excited that he was going to get to show off for his friend again, and he was thrilled about doing a good deed for some of the "ground-pounders" stationed at a lonely outpost just northeast of Bien Hoa. As they got up from the little table in the club, he kept up the chatter about how these guys needed something special, and how Terry and he should come up with something special for them.

Terry was a captain, but Ski had been in country for over four months and that made him an Old Timer. Terry had only been in country for seven weeks. They were a lot alike. Terry was a little slimmer than Ski, but they were both about six feet tall, and in their dark green Nomex flight suits, they looked a lot alike anyway. Well, everyone looked alike in their suits—and nobody had much hair. army regs prohibited beards or mustaches, and haircuts were super-close.

* * *

Down in the company operations shack was an underground bunker accessed by a switchback stairway and a tunnel. That's where Specialist Hull was found. It took a special kind of guy to sit around listening to radios all day and checking pilots in an out. But the job had its perks. To keep the electronics stable, the room had to be kept cool, so it was just about the coolest place in the company area. Hull was short and had a pot belly, and because he had a lot of dead time between radio calls, he did a lot of reading. He was normally found sitting behind the operations desk with his feet up, book in hand. There just wasn't much else to do.

For some reason he had a passion for Shakespeare, and he was always uttering obscure lines. The pilots had nicknamed him "Puck." They'd come in and get their gear—survival pack, personal emergency radio, and an SOI, which contained the codes for secure communications. No one was sure, but it was rumored that the VC got copies of the codes before the pilots did.

On the wall next to the dispatch window was a blackboard with the day's missions written in chalk. Ski had already been down, and he knew where he was to go today. He knew he didn't have to carry an observer, so the back seat was free. Puck gave him his gear. Ski put the string attached to the SOI book around his neck and stuck the white, stiff book in his left breast pocket. He strapped the survival kit and radio to his right leg and fastened it securely in place with a wide Velcro band, a little like a gunfighter from the Old West tying down his holster.

"I need some more .45 ammo," said Ski.

"What do you do with it all," asked Puck.

"I shoot things," Ski replied with a chuckle. "Isn't that what war is all about? You know—kill people and break things?"

Puck bent down under the counter and came up with a small box. Then with dramatic pause and a sweeping gesture of his hand he said, "Now, by heaven, my blood begins my safer guides to rule, and passion, having my best judgment collied, assays to lead the way." He handed the ammo to the rather puzzled Ski. "Here's a full box," he said softly, "but you have to sign for it."

"Heck of a deal—I have to sign for bullets. You'd think we were stateside, wouldn't you," Ski replied with a little sarcasm. "Hey, as long as I'm here, give me a box of tracers, too. By the way, who the hell was that you were quoting that time, Puck?"

"Othello. Nice, huh? I was just waiting for the right time to use it. I'm glad I didn't waste it on Captain Mac, that cranky—"

"Hold it, Specialist—he's still an officer."

"Yeah, and a bit of a shithead, if you ask me." Ski and Terry tried to stifle chuckle.

The radio crackled. "Aloft Base, this is Aloft Four-Five, do you read?"

Puck picked up the mike hanging next to the UHF radio mounted on the wall. "Aloft Four-Five, this is Base, go ahead," he replied. Now he was all business, calm, professional. No Shakespeare.

As Ski and Terry left the bunker, they could hear Aloft Four-Five reporting his position and estimated time of return. It was nice to know that someone was listening, keeping a record of where you were supposed to be. Puck was like the mother hen that kept track of all the chicks. He never got any flak from them. The pilots looked out for him too.

Spec Four Andrew Beck, one of the company clerks, passed them going down as the two were climbing the stairs and leaving the bunker. "How you doin', A-Sap?" Ski asked as they passed. It was funny how names stuck. Beck didn't seem to mind, but that nickname bothered Terry. Beck was a bit special, not very bright, and very quiet, as if he held everything in. And he moved kind of slow, like he was moving at his own pace. Hence the nickname, ASAP. But he was diligent in his work, and Terry just never liked people making fun of others for their perceived shortcomings. He did wonder, though, how the guy ever got in the army.

From down below, Terry heard Puck's voice as though he'd just entered stage right. "Alas, here comes my messenger. How now, mad spirit." Terry just shook his head.

* * *

The sky was clear and the air was still. The sun had risen an hour before and a hint of sunrise colors still clung with quiet passion to the distant horizon. Terry thought that such things were special to pilots. Ordinary people don't get to see all of nature's wondrous beauty like a pilot does. Even in a war zone there was awesome beauty to be found.

Ski keyed the intercom and spoke. "That's it up there. You see that mound with the little tower like shed on top? That's it."

Terry strained to see around Ski and out the front windshield. He saw a small conical shaped hill, about 260–270 feet high, sticking out of the otherwise flat countryside. Around the hill the jungle was cleared away for about two to three miles in every direction.

Terry spoke into his helmet-mounted mike. "Not much to look at, is it . . ."

"No, not much, but that's Alphie—Alpha Base One," he replied.

The little post was just a tin shed on top of a very small hill, and the six guys who manned it had to keep their eyes and ears open twenty-four hours a day, looking for enemy troop movements and monitoring radios for long-range reconnaissance patrols that were in the nearby jungles. Because of its elevation, it was easy to see the few miles out to where the triple canopy jungle began. But it also made it an easy target for an enemy who could hide just inside the jungle perimeter and come out at night to lob mortars on an unprotected target.

Over time, they'd dug a cave-like bunker inside the hill and sandbagged the entrance. They'd put concertina and barbed wire around the base of the hill and laid out a mine field. But even with all the precautions and fortifications, "vulnerable" was the word that best described their position—vulnerable and lonely. They only got to leave for a short time every two or three months. A helicopter would bring them food once a week but it was mainly cold rations.

For some reason, Ski knew how they must have felt—even though he'd never set foot inside their compound. He had great compassion and wanted to help any way he could—and if anyone could use a little Christmas cheer, it was surely the guys on Alphie.

Inside the bunkered mound were sleeping quarters and a dining room that doubled as a recreation room. Not much there—just a table and some board games, and a makeshift bookshelf with a lot of paperback books and old dog-eared *Playboy* magazines. They stood shifts in the lookout shack at the top of the hill—

typically four hours on and eight off. So sometimes they'd be on shift in the day and then later at night. That way it stayed fair for everyone, although it made it hard to develop a sleep routine.

Sgt. Gus Jacobson was the current NCOIC of the post, and he liked having things fair. He felt there were worse places he and his men could be—like out in the jungle on patrol and not being able to see where the enemy was coming from. Yes, they were a little like sitting ducks, but the US had air superiority, and they were a small target for mortars or RPGs. So relatively speaking, their odds were maybe just a little better than those poor guys out on patrol . . . maybe.

Gus had gone up to the lookout shack when he was told a Bird Dog was flying by. He peered up as the nose of the Bird Dog pointed downward.

In the plane, Terry's stomach lurched as Ski keyed his mike and said, "I'm going to fly by and wave hello. I do that a lot when I'm in the area. I think it makes 'em feel that someone's lookin' out for 'em." The altimeter reeled off the descending numbers: 3,000, 2500, 1500, 500, and then leveled off at 300 feet, just about level with the top of the hill called Alphie.

Ski reached up to the FM radio located in the wing root above and to the left of his head and dialed in 40.50 megahertz. He switched his control panel to transmit and keyed his mike. "Alphie, this is Aloft Three-Two. How're you guys doin' today?"

Gus picked up the base radio mike. "Hey, three-two, is that you flyin' by? Good to see you. See any Charlies out there?"

"Nah, just checkin' up on you," radioed Ski. "You still got six happy troops?"

"Sure do, but we'd be a lot happier if we could get home for Christmas. We'd even settle for a little time in the barracks at Bien Hoa." He sighed, and Ski and Terry could hear his loneliness.

"Listen," said Ski, "we're working on a little surprise for you. We'll try to bring it out in the next few days, in time for Christmas anyway. But we gotta go now. Duty calls."

"Yeah, right. You pilots really lead the life. You probably even have an air-conditioned hooch, right?"

"See you next time, out," replied Ski, avoiding the question.

"Roger, out," replied the sergeant.

Ski waved the wings and rudder as he made his second flyby of the small mound of earth. Terry could count four guys out in front of the little shack, waving as the airplane passed within about fifty feet of the hill. Terry figured the other two must be down in the bunker sleeping.

* * *

It was three days before Christmas when the little Bird Dog took off again for Alphie. Aboard was a package with a special parachute that Ski and Terry had built at some risk to their personal reputations. When they'd gone out into the company yard to test it, a couple of the other pilots laughed at them. They tested it by standing on top of a CONEX container and throwing their chute into the air to see if it would open. The other guys didn't understand what was going on—they just ridiculed their friends. But the test had worked, sort of. All it had to do was break the fall enough so that the two bottles of Mateus wouldn't break. Terry had begged two loaves of bread from the mess hall, and they'd hollowed out the inside and inserted the bottles. Hopefully the bread would provide just enough cushioning for the bottles to survive. The cookies they were sending would survive the drop just fine. Christmas was on its way to Alphie.

* * *

It was December 22nd, and there were a lot of puffy white clouds building in the skies north of Bien Hoa. The Bird Dog and its two pilot comrades were heading back toward Alphie.

Tim Ewell

Ski said in his best bomber-pilot imitation, "Approaching the target."

"Roger, target in sight," Terry replied formally. Then he said, "Don't you think you better call them so they can try to catch this thing?"

"Yeah," said Ski, switching to transmit. "Alphie, this is Aloft Three-Two, we've got a surprise for you. It'll be on its way shortly. By the way, we've never done this before, so keep your eyes open—we're dropping a package."

Two guys appeared, then a third, then all six were outside the observation shack. Ski said to Terry, "Now just like we talked about. I'll put it into a stall right over 'em and you pitch it out the window. Ready?"

"Ready as I'll ever be," Terry replied.

Terry had the back window open. The package just barely fit through. He heard the engine cut back and felt the Bird Dog slow down. Then he heard Ski say, "Now—were right over 'em." Terry pushed the package out. The little chute was wrapped on top, and he held onto the top of it to help it unfurl. The package fell as it was supposed to and went under the horizontal stabilizer, but as soon as the wind caught the chute, it filled and pulled out of his hand. The airflow took it over the stabilizer while the package went under, and the whole works was caught, chute inflated above and package hanging below. It immediately caused the airplane to yaw hard to the left.

"What's going on?" yelled Ski.

"The chute's hung up on the tail," Terry yelled back, a little panic in his voice.

"Well get it loose—I can hardly control this thing."

Terry reached out the window, back to where the chute had become entangled. He couldn't reach far enough to grab it. "Get it loose, *now*!" yelled Ski as he gunned the engine to regain airspeed.

Terry realized this was bad. He turned and faced forward. *Think—what can I do? I can't reach back that far out of the window, even with my seat belt off.* He saw the back seat control stick between his legs just in front of him and had an idea. The pilot had the main control stick, but there was also one in back for the observer or copilot. But the back seat stick was held in by a single pin at the base. Terry hurriedly reached down and pulled out the pin and yanked upward on the two-and-a-half-foot stick. It came out in his hand.

Ski was still a bit panicked, trying to maintain control of the plane. Somehow they'd managed to stay over Alphie. Terry reached out the window with the control stick in his hand. But it still wasn't far enough. He unfastened his seat belt and leaned way out. Now he could just reach the parachute cords. He pushed them outward toward the tip of the stabilizer, and the air currents caught the chute and it flipped over. The whole thing slid off the stabilizer and parachuted much too quickly to the ground.

"Got it loose," Terry reported over the intercom as he sat back in his seat and fastened his seat belt. "I felt like I was about to fall out there for a minute." He replaced the control stick in its socket and reinserted the locking pin.

"That's all we'd need," said Ski with relief in his voice. "Can you imagine me explaining that to the CO? 'Well, Sir, he was leaning out the window of the airplane trying to get this Christmas package off the tail, and that's the last I saw of him.'"

"Funny, Ski, real funny. But it's nice to know we think alike. Did you see it land?" said Terry.

"No. I'll call Alphie and see if they saw it." He keyed his mike. "Alphie, do you read me?"

"Yeah, Aloft, we read you. Nice job. You put it in the mine field. And it hit pretty hard. Your parachute didn't work too good." His voice was heavy with sarcasm.

"Yeah, now they probably have cookie powder for Christmas," mumbled Terry.

"If they're not real careful, it'll be exploding cookie powder," said Ski.

"Soaked in Mateus," Terry said. "Tell me again why I fly with you."

"Well, it was for a good cause, and we tried," said Ski. "Hey—know what? I'm going up to the orphanage in a couple of days, wanna go with me?"

"I'm not sure you and me and a Bird Dog are the best idea right now," replied Terry.

"No, no—we'll take a Jeep. It's only about ten or twelve miles. You'll love the kids. Pop can't go, so it'll be just you and me." He paused, then added, "Not to worry. The VC stay clear of that area. They think it's bad luck to mess with the nuns."

"Let me think about it," said Terry. "You and me in a Beaver. That was a fun time, right?" he added sarcastically. "This was sure a lot of laughs, too. Now you want me to go somewhere with you in a Jeep? Let's just get back home and not tell anyone about this fiasco, okay?"

* * *

The next day Ski called Alphie as he was outbound for his mission. "You guys ever get our present?" he asked.

"No problem," came the reply. The cookies were great, hardly broken, and we're saving the Mateus for Christmas day. Oh, and the *Playboy* you used to wrap the cookies was a big hit. Thanks for the trouble, and Merry Christmas. By the way, what happened to your copilot?'

Ski keyed his mike. "He decided he'd do his own flying for a while. Said he was going to work on finding something sane to accomplish, like flying by himself for a change. By the way, if you talk to him, don't mention the *Playboy*. I kind of borrowed it from his roommate."

Ski flew on northeast, climbing into the morning sun. Just another day over South Vietnam. What would this day hold? His hand felt for his shoulder holster and the Model 1911 Colt .45 semi-automatic pistol inside. His fingers felt the roughness of the crosscut grip. Every third round was a tracer. It was very little assurance up here all alone, but it was something. Having a friend on board was better, but this would have to do for now. Ahead he could see where the Dong Nai River curved and headed south. He'd spent a lot of time looking at landmarks from the air and wondered if he'd ever have to use that knowledge to help him find his way out of the jungle if he were ever shot down or crashed.

Chapter 7

There are certain events in a pilot's life that remain crystal clear. At least they seemed crystal clear to Terry. A lot of those events, those he recalled as if they were yesterday, involved flying.

On one particular day back when he was in flight training at Ft. Rucker, not more than 6 months ago, Terry was with his flight school classmates as they arrived by shuttle bus to Cairns Army Air Field, where they would receive their introduction to the O-1 Bird Dog aircraft. "O" stands for observation, and since it was the only fixed-wing observation aircraft the army had, Terry guessed the number "one" summed it all up. Up to this point they had all received their introduction to flying in the T-41, a Cessna four-place training aircraft, and they'd completed instrument training and multi-engine training in the Beechcraft T-42, which was a modified Beechcraft Baron, Model 55. Terry had been a pilot before joining the army and had already accumulated about eighty hours of flight time in various planes, but mostly in his dad's Piper Cherokee. Over the last five months, the army had added 150 more hours to that civilian time, and it was all intensive, specialized training.

The class of rookies walked from the bus to the flight line where there were a whole line up of Bird Dog's lined up next to a grass landing strip.

All the aircraft Terry had flown up to now had certain things in common. For one, they had tricycle gear—a wheel under each wing and one under the nose. The Bird Dog was different. It was called a tail-dragger because while it had wheels under the wing, the third wheel was under the tail. So instead of sitting level when you got into the cockpit, in a Bird Dog you sat at an angle, looking upward. The engine cowl obscured much of the pilot's forward vision while it was on the ground, and the tail wheel made it more difficult to handle.

The lead instructor began telling the group of pilots who had gathered around him about the characteristics of their new aircraft.

First there was the control stick. In the other aircraft Terry had flown, the stick was a stick in name only. It was more like a steering wheel that came out of the dash, which you pushed in and out to go down and up and turned it side to side, like the steering wheel on a car, to make it bank left and right. The Bird Dog, on the other hand, had a real "stick"—a gray-green tube of metal with a black plastic handle at the top that came up between the pilot's legs from the center of the floorboard. On the handle were a red "trigger" mechanism and a little round thumb button that keyed the mike.

There was something else about this plane. Because it had a very narrow fuselage, the pilot and instructor—or pilot and observer, when flying missions—didn't sit side-by-side. Instead the pilot sat in front and the instructor or observer sat in back. This, incidentally, afforded the pilot a great view of the ground because he could look out either side of the plane. But as a trainer, this was a disadvantage, because most of the engine controls and switches were in the front, and all the instructor had were a throttle, flap switch, and a stick. If a student pilot screwed up, it was almost impossible for the instructor to reach the mag switch and other controls. That was one of the reasons that they didn't start pilots off training in that aircraft. There were just too many ways a rookie could make a mistake.

After the brief orientation, each student pilot was given an instructor and after the introductions they walked over to their assigned aircraft to get ready to fly.

Terry and his instructor, Lt. Bellwether, were finishing their preflight inspection as another crew was starting to taxi out to the runway. All of a sudden their engine roared and their little O-1 started spinning around in a circle, like a dog chasing its tail. "Ground loop", said Bellwether matter-of-factly. "He's simulating one. Shows how squirrelly tail draggers are. You have to fly 'em even when they're on the ground, or they can get away from you."

Once they were aboard their plane, engine started and beginning to taxi, Bellwether pointed to a patch of grass off to the right. "I've got it," he said and took control of the aircraft. They already had clearance to take off at their own discretion. It was considered a training launch—the first aircraft called for clearance, and the rest followed as they were ready. Twenty-seven aircraft, one after the other, pointed their noses down the green grass runway and headed out for the day's training. Bellwether pointed the plane out onto the grass and pushed the throttle full forward. The Bird Dog was small, but it made up for it with the power of a larger aircraft. It had a whopping 245 horsepower, almost double that of a comparable civilian aircraft.

The engine surged to full power in just a few feet. Bellwether pushed the stick forward, and the tail came off the ground, raised them up, and planted the aircraft on its two front wheels. After only another 300 feet or so, the instructor pulled gently back on the stick and the aircraft almost jumped into the air. "Well, off like a dirty shirt," Bellwether said over the intercom, and they banked left and headed for their first destination, Skelly, a small field without a control tower. It was an intermediate training field about fifteen miles away.

As soon as they were pointed in the right direction and climbing gently, Bellwether said, "Okay, you got it." Terry gripped the stick in his right hand and reached for the throttle with his left, and they were on their way. It felt a little awkward at first, but within moments, Terry was thinking that it felt very natural. Controlling a stick-type aircraft is more natural than a control-wheel type. To him it felt right, like this was the way a plane should be flown. No wonder high-performance jets all had sticks. *It's how a plane should be designed*, he thought.

Terry brought his mind back to the mission at hand. He was wondering why that particular memory had stuck with him. He really didn't know. There was just something about being up in the front seat in that plane with someone sitting behind him. He thought it might be like being in the front seat of a roller coaster, although he'd never been on one. Something about "firsts" usually sticks in everyone's memory. The Bird Dog was a great airplane, so it was no surprise that his first ride was memorable.

Terry thought the training was probably harder than the combat missions—for him anyway. There was less margin for error than in the kind of in country flying they really did. They were trained to fly into and out of small dirt strips, some surrounded by tall trees, some uphill or next to a cliff. And the instructor was always shutting off the fuel, which made the engine quit, then saying, "Okay, you just lost your engine. Where you gonna put it?" And they would have to simulate a forced landing by gliding to the nearest appropriate landing spot.

His mind wandered back to flight school again.

Probably the most difficult area of training, the one that caused more pilots to wash out, was low-level flying, where they had to plan a flight, take off, and fly no higher than fifty feet above the terrain. They had to navigate by using time, distance, and landmarks without instruments. They had to get to various points, turn toward a new point, find it, then fly on to the next until it was the last leg, and then return them to base. It was Terry's favorite part of flight school.

He remembered the story of one of the instructors in that phase, Capt. Bob Richards. He'd nearly been killed in Vietnam. He was the first pilot to be hit by a radar-controlled .50 caliber machine gun, and who lived to tell about it. The round that got him came up through the engine, through the firewall, through the dash, and hit him in the middle of the sternum. It nearly knocked him out, but if it hadn't been slowed down by everything it passed through, it would surely have killed him.

Terry believed the captain's story would save lives. Richards explained it was about the beep-beep he'd heard on his FM radio, just seconds before he was hit. It was the sound of the radar controlled .50-caliber machine gun locking its radar onto the target. If he could describe this sound to others, and if they heard that sound and acted quickly enough, maybe they could take evasive action and get out of the "lock." He had a medical profile now. Because of his injury, he would never have to go back to Vietnam, but he could train others—and he was good at it too.

It got hot at Fort Rucker, Alabama. Not as hot as here in Vietnam. It was not even hot enough to simulate some of the conditions they'd find when they flew in the war zone. Things like flying with both the side windows open, using the window sills as arm rests, like when you were driving a car. Whoever heard of flying an airplane like that? It didn't seem right to Terry at first. The windows were hinged at the top, and when the catch was released they swung up toward the wing. There was a catch on the wing to hold it in place, but it was only needed on the ground. Aloft, the air pressure held the window up in place. Sometimes the catch didn't work, and when the aircraft came in for a landing and the air pressure dropped, the window would fall and hit the pilot on the elbow. In training, they had to leave the sleeves of their Nomex flight suits rolled down all the time—and it was hotter that way. It was to protect them in case of fire. They were supposed to do that in Vietnam too, but few ever did. As soon as they got off the ground and away from the eyes of higher ups and safety officers, they rolled up their sleeves and rested their arms out the open windows. It was a lot more comfortable that way.

Recon Airplane Company: III Corps, Vietnam

* * *

But here he was, in III Corps. He wasn't getting as much sleep as he would like. It was hard to sleep in the day time, in the heat. Then there were the night missions. Flying Lerp watch was boring. Each of the pilots on the Lerp team was averaging 150–175 hours flying time per month. And when you consider preflight time, refueling, briefings, paperwork, and the rest of the military crap, there wasn't a whole lot of time to sleep.

So Terry developed a technique, and later he'd discover that he wasn't the only one who took advantage of it. If he was flying at night and didn't have an observer in the back seat, and if nothing was happening on the ground, he would sleep—all alone, no autopilot, no copilot. He wouldn't sleep for long, but long enough that he felt more refreshed than if he hadn't. The technique involved the proper position.

In a Bird Dog, the back of the seat was supposed to be a parachute. But parachutes were hard and uncomfortable, to say the least. The aircraft in Vietnam had nice, foam seat cushions—at least the ones in this RAC Company did. Somebody with a lot of common sense decided that, with the amount of flying the pilots were doing, it might be better if they had comfortable seats. After all, no one ever bailed out of an aircraft like this, so a parachute was more or less a useless piece of feel-good equipment—just bureaucratic nonsense that someone who knew nothing about airplanes decided would save lives. In fact, it could do just the opposite. So they had special foam inserts constructed that fit into the bullet-proof seats. Now, if Terry scrunched down in the seat, he could suspend his legs by resting his knees up on the instrument panel in front of him.

Being six-one made it easier. He could reach down to the trim wheel at his left side and trim the airplane into a very gentle climb, then let go of the controls and relax. Most nights the air was smooth as glass, and it was almost like being on autopilot.

As soon as he let go of the rudders and the stick, the plane would go into a slow climbing turn to the left. With his head resting on the soft seat-back cushion, he'd fall asleep. He always turned up the volume on the radio receiver tuned to the Lerps and their headquarters in case they called, and he'd wake up.

Terry had flown this AO (Area of Operations) so often that whenever he woke up, he could look around and quickly know where he was. He knew where all the teams were by number and location on the ground, so if they called he could quickly maneuver his aircraft above them.

The only other procedure a Bird Dog pilot had to follow was fuel management. An O-1 has two fuel tanks, one in each wing. In some aircraft, the fuel selector has a "both" position, and the engine can run off both tanks at the same time. But this is not the case in a Bird Dog. In order to keep the airplane properly balanced, the rule was to switch tanks every thirty minutes. It seemed like Terry had a sixth sense for that. He would wake up every thirty minutes and reach into the left wing root where the valve was located and change tanks. Then after a minute or two and after checking the engine instruments and the altitude, he'd be back asleep.

Besides a call from the Lerps or the automatic thirty-minute wakeup, there was another reason a pilot sat up straight, and that was when the engine started to run rough. That was usually caused by spark plugs fouled from running the engine at a lower RPM than normal on flights like this. But normally Terry got a lot of much-appreciated sleep—and as far as he knew, it was his secret, and he was the only one who did it. At least he deluded himself into believing that.

Chapter 8

Before the Americans went into Vietnam, there were the French. After all, it was their colony. It was all about the Michelin rubber plantations—vast areas of former jungle turned into row upon row of tall, jade green, shiny-leafed trees that filled great areas of the country.

Before synthetic rubber was developed, these trees supplied much of the world's rubber. And tires, the primary use for rubber, were in even greater demand in the years following WWII. A boon for the French economy, rubber production meant great wealth. Labor was cheap, production costs were low, and the profits were magnificent. In addition to rubber, the region was perfect for growing rice. It was a food basket for a large part of that region of the world. It was no wonder the French wanted to retain control. But as in any society where a ruling class takes the lion's share of the land's bounty while others live on the scraps that trickle down, there would be change. If the people of the region did not revolt, neighboring countries would covet the wealth and try to steal it.

What little industrialization there was in Vietnam was introduced by the French. The city of Saigon may have existed prior to the arrival of the French, but the French rebuilt the heart of it in their architectural style. Most of the villages had government office buildings built by the French. And the plantation manors were as opulent as the antebellum architecture of Louisiana, which was also once controlled by the French.

And where there were government offices and plantations, there were soldiers and policeman to maintain order and protect

Tim Ewell

the vital economic interest of the investing country. Here too, the French were in primary control.

It was in the village of Tay Ninh that they posted Corporal Jean Pierre Montaigne. At twenty–three, he was not the youngest soldier, but he was still pretty young. He was tall, with dark hair that was close cut in a military fashion. He had sharp, yet not unpleasant facial features, and a strong chin. He was very trim and fit. His uniform fit him like the poster boy in a recruitment ad. But his most memorable features were his eyes. They were a piercing steel blue, like those of a Siberian husky.

Tay Ninh is located in the southwestern part of the country, with the border of Cambodia and Laos not far away. One prominent landscape feature is visible from the city—a dormant volcanic mountain called Nui Ba Din, rising 4,000 feet from the jungle floor. Tay Ninh was not much of a place in the early days—mostly just shanties and a couple of government buildings. The government buildings looked a lot alike. They were made of clay bricks coated with stucco and painted white. Because of the equatorial climate, the paint would mildew and require frequent repainting, and most buildings looked like their paint was peeling. Jean worked in one of these buildings. There really wasn't a lot to do—it was just that his presence was needed. The locals were very cooperative and, for the most part, passive. The province chief lived in the village in a house that had been built for him by the local plantation owner. It gave the chief great status, and helped to secure his favor in the local political situations that might arise.

Most towns like this had a large center street, which was lined with the people's homes. Some were built with brick and plaster like the French buildings, but most of them were unpainted. Some were just wood and whatever scraps that could be found. They were a patchwork of old corrugated tin and thatch and boards. In this climate, walls were not all that important. The weather almost never turned cold enough to be uncomfortable. The main protection afforded by the walls and thatched roofs was against the torrential seasonal rains, which could last just a few minutes or as long as an hour, but could deliver several inches of water. In the front and back were pens for animals, but the pens really didn't do a lot of good. Many of the animals wandered the streets and went into houses and just about anywhere they pleased. But nobody seemed to pay much attention. This included forays into the government office, where Jean spent a modest amount of time tossing out a stray chicken or driving out a roaming goat.

Jean lived in a barracks behind the government office with five other soldiers. It was a simple, rectangular building with a four-foot brick-and-mortar wall. Up from the wall were framed screens that went up another four feet. These were in place to let a little breeze into the room and still keep the critters out. The whole thing was covered with a heavy thatched roof. Inside were six bunks, each covered with mosquito netting, and in the center of the room there was a small sitting area with a large radio. The radio stood on four legs and had a large dial in the center. It looked like something from another era, but it had its use. It had more receiving power than the newer, smaller radios, and it could receive broadcasts on higher frequencies. It was a vacuum–tube radio, so it took a few minutes to warm up, but it was a way to stay in touch with home. In the evening, when things were just right, they could pick up broadcasts from other countries—including their homeland, France.

Each man had a personal area around his bunk, with personal photos, a black wooden footlocker, and various local souvenirs. The footlocker was each soldier's private area, and no one violated anyone else's privacy. It was where you kept your valuables and things like letters from home.

Like many areas of the world, Vietnam was a country that you either loved or hated. It wasn't so much the people as it was the climate. Some people were born for warm climates, while others loved the cold. Jean loved the steamy jungle heat. His five roommates hated it. And Jean really liked the people—he had a winning way with them. They seemed to have a mutual understanding. Whenever the local French constable had a disagreement with the local village chief, he would call upon Jean to sit in and try to help settle the situation. More often than not, Jean had a way of explaining things to both sides that helped them reach a compromise. It was at one of these meetings that he saw Xuan Do for the first time.

She was with her father, a village chief from Dau Tieng. They'd come to Tay Ninh for a meeting of regional leaders to discuss labor issues and the growing unrest coming from outside areas. She stood beside her father with her head bowed slightly as he spoke to the French regional governor, who was in town to oversee the meeting. His was a courtesy visit, just to meet and say hello before the official meeting. Jean and his five comrades were dressed in their best and all were on duty together for the next couple of days while the meeting took place. Although he was taken by Xuan Do's quiet beauty, Jean maintained his military bearing and stood looking mostly straight ahead. Occasionally, he would steal a glance in her direction. Most Vietnamese girls were much shorter than he was, and most were slightly stooped. Xuan Do was much taller, perhaps five-foot-seven, and stood straighter, and her dark, black hair was neatly brushed long and straight.

The meeting was to last several days, and it would of course include banquets in honor of the special guests. Tonight's banquet was in the home of the local village chief. All the local and visiting dignitaries were invited. Two French Legionnaires stood by the front door, dressed in their sparkling pressed white uniforms. They would assure that only invited guests were allowed in—and while they were at it keep stray chickens and dogs from wandering in. Because Jean was so well acquainted with the local officials, he was invited to serve as the governor's aide for the banquet.

After the customary introductions and social amenities, everyone was seated at a long table. Jean sat to the right of the governor, who sat at the head of the table. That permitted the governor to quietly ask Jean questions so that he would be best prepared to handle all situations. As luck would have it, Xuan Do was seated on Jean's right.

Although she was not fluent in French, Xuan Do had attended a local school sponsored by her local plantation manager. As the daughter of a village chief, she was afforded some privileges, and her father felt it important that she be able to understand the foreigner's language. He had no sons, and he held his daughter in great esteem. It was for her language skills that he brought her along. She would listen to the conversations and later try to explain to her father things he may have missed, or may have been said as an aside that he was not intended to hear. He was a wise man who was interested in giving his people a descent life. He was well regarded among his peers and by the French.

After some initial polite table talk, the meal began. The conversation at the table subsided, and it gave Jean time to speak to the lovely stranger seated beside him. As with most Vietnamese girls, she was very shy. She spoke with only short answers to his questions, and always avoided eye contact. Her French was quite acceptable, and he could tell she understood much more than she let on. Although she remained shy, he could tell that she was not afraid of him and actually enjoyed the conversation. As the evening went on and the meal continued, she spoke somewhat more freely. Jean, in his two years in country, had learned some Vietnamese. It was one of the things that helped in his relations with the people and why they took to him so well. When he would switch from French to Vietnamese, he could see a little twinkle in Xuan Do's eyes. His charm was working.

Actually, she'd heard about him from the local village chief, having inquired about him after the brief introductory meeting earlier with the governor. He had explained that this Frenchman was different. He loved the country and its people. He was a friend who could be trusted in a general sense. They knew he was also loyal to his country and his superiors.

Xuan Do had never met anyone like Jean. He seemed confident, yet kind. He was not like some of the others who had tried to push themselves on her. He was patient. This was a most important trait, one most foreigners didn't understand. French life was a life of daily achievements, with goals and quotas. Hers was a life of existence, based on the seasons, when crops were planted and harvested, and when animals migrated through their part of the countryside.

After the banquet, in the short time before the guests departed, Jean asked her if he might call upon her the next day at noon. She hesitated, then shyly agreed.

When he got back to his quarters that evening, his buddies began with the questions. He merely laughed. "It's just keeping up the local relations," he told them, and went to bed. He usually fell right to sleep, while others had a difficult time in the jungle heat. But tonight it was he who wrestled with sleep. A couple of mosquitoes kept buzzing overhead his bunk, and his mind lingered on Xuan Do's beauty.

* * *

How all of it came together is a story in itself. There was the courtship, the approvals from the locals and the French authorities, and the understanding of his family back home. But it happened, and they were married. He maintained his duties, and she moved in with him in a small, one-room home that he managed to have built a short distance from the offices. About a year later she became pregnant. They were both delighted.

As the French moved out of Vietnam and were replaced by Americans, some were allowed to stay behind. Jean Pierre mustered out of the military and was quickly hired by one of the remaining plantation owners as an overseer. It just so happened it was near Dau Tieng, which allowed them to be close to Xuan Do's father. The baby came later that year. Yes, he had mostly Vietnamese features, but he had his father's blue eyes. When the baby was only two years old, the plantation owners were forced out by rebels. Xuan Do's father was brutally killed, but she and Jean managed to escape to the east along jungle paths, traveling with a few others who feared they too would be killed if they remained.

* * *

That was over six years ago, more than five years since the baby was born. They had found jobs at other plantations in various places, but they had to stay on the move. They'd recently found a home in a small village just a few miles north of Phu Loi. They liked the smaller village because there were fewer questions asked and fewer to answer. They never told the story of her heritage. Xuan Do was good at pulling her own weight around the village. Her language skills proved helpful on several occasions. Together their training in diplomacy helped to defuse a couple of tense situations between the villagers and the rogue VC, who came by regularly for supplies and information. But two weeks ago it didn't work. A particularly brutal group of VC came through the village, and when they spotted Jean they pulled him out into the street and began to beat him with their rifles. His well-spoken Vietnamese language skills were of no use.

Xuan Do had quietly taken their boy and headed into the jungle. When she saw the VC leader pull out his pistol and shoot her husband in the head, it was like someone ripping out her heart. All she could do now was try to save herself and their precious son.

Tim Ewell

When the villagers found her, lying silent on the path leading into the jungle, they were filled with remorse. She had been such a help to them and such a willing worker. They also were concerned for her son. But after a couple of days of searching, they assumed he too had been killed by the VC.

Chapter 9

It was just Lt. Johnson, Britman, Doc, and a six-year-old boy in the hooch. Doc held the boy with the bandage on his head on his lap. There was a lot of frustration in the air.

"No, we can't!" shouted the lieutenant.

"But, Sir," the sergeant said in a calm voice, "what chance does he have without us?"

"That doesn't matter. We can't just make him our mascot and have him running around camp. Somebody is bound to say something, and then we'll all be in trouble."

"I wasn't talking about making him a mascot, Sir. I just thought . . . well, look at him, Sir. Just look at him. If the VC get this kid, he's dead. And I for one—

The sound of a battery of 155 mm howitzers firing together ended the sentence with a deafening boom as they sent a volley out into the nearby jungle. Brit was upset, but remained calm. The interruption forced him to stop and think. He wasn't getting anywhere. They'd been back at base camp for two days. The little blue-eyed boy had come back with them, and Brit had put him in his tent. Doc had helped him look after him. He had a nasty knot on the back of his head, and a gash on top of it where the skin had split, but otherwise he seemed all right. They'd brought soup from the mess hall for him, and were giving him Kool-Aid and Coke. He was getting his strength back.

During the day, other team members would drop in and check on his progress, and sometimes bring him some food or something they'd made for him. One of them had carved him a top and tried to show him how to wind the string around it and toss it onto the ground and make it spin. All the guys did their best to look out for him. Brit saw to it that the boy was never left alone, and today, for the first time, he seemed a little relaxed. Every now and then he'd say something in Vietnamese, but no one could make it out, and they were not about to ask a hooch maid to interpret for them. This secret had to be close-held for now.

It quieted down, and Brit turned back to face the lieutenant. "I guess you're right, Sir—it's just that, well . . . I really feel something special for this kid. I don't know exactly why. Maybe it's the blue eyes. Maybe it's just that he's one good part of a bad experience, and I'd like to find a way to hang on to that good feeling."

Johnson's face softened. He took a deep breath and puffed out his cheeks as he let it out. "Listen, Brit. You know how I feel about you and all the guys in our squad. We've been through too much not to know about how we each think . . . react—but this . . . this is more than we can deal with. But I'll tell you what I'll do. We've got three more days before we go back in."

"Sir, I want to try to—"

"Don't interrupt me, Brit. I'm going to give you two days to find a solution. On Tuesday, I take over and we do a report and go through channels—the whole nine yards. Got it?"

"Yes, Sir."

Britman turned to leave, stopped at the door and turned around. "Sir, can you get me a Jeep for tomorrow? I'll need it most of the day."

The lieutenant thought for a moment. "I'll see what I can do." He turned to leave, then turned back again. "No, better yet—just tell Sgt. Klein in the motor pool I have a job for you and to give you my Jeep. Now get outta here. And Brit? Take good care of the kid."

* * *

It was Sunday, but in the Vietnam war zone, the days were all alike. There were no special days, and no weekends off. *Tomorrow*, Brit thought, *I'll drive down into the village and see if I can find a family that will take the kid and give him a home.* It was the best he could do. But now, he decided, he needed to go to the base PX and see what was new. Maybe there'd be something there that would give him an idea. Anyway, it would be a good break. Doc was watching the kid, and he needed some time to think.

It was another muggy day. Like most everyone else, Britman's jungle fatigues were soaked with sweat under the arms and around the collar. It wasn't a long walk to the PX, but any exertion on a day like this sapped your strength.

The PX wasn't much to look at—just a stubby frame building with a corrugated metal roof, and it was only big enough for ten or fifteen people at a time. Brit had to stand in line and wait his turn to go in. Luckily, the line wasn't long. While he stood in line, two pilots in Nomex flight suits came up and stood behind him. The two pilots were engaged in conversation. He couldn't help but overhear what they were saying.

"Ski, I don't know. Driving even a few miles north seems a little risky to me. Going south to Saigon, now that's no big deal. But driving north?"

"No problem. We do it all the time, me and Pop."

"Don't you worry about the VC? . . . I mean, we're used to being up and away. This ground stuff is a little scary."

Brit chuckled to himself. *Pilots. They probably even have air-conditioned hooches.* The line moved forward as two soldiers came out and two were allowed to go in.

"Terry, you've been flying the Lerps quite a bit lately, right?"

"Right."

Brit's interest was piqued when he heard the word "Lerp."

"Well, you know what we need to take up to the orphanage? Some Lerp rations. The kids would get a kick out of that. How do you think we can get a case?"

"Why do you always go out of your way to create these special missions?" Terry said to Ski.

"Wait till you see the place, and the faces of the kids. Then you'll understand," Ski replied. "I know—let's ask Pop."

"Pop?"

"Duh—of course. Wonder where he is today? Is he flying the Moon River or—"

"Excuse me, Sir," interrupted Sgt. Britman. "You guys are Lerp pilots?"

"That's right," said Ski, "among other things. You a Lerp?"

"Yes, Sir, I am, Britman acknowledged. "Just got in from the field a couple of days ago. Lately we've been working in the area north of Xuan Loc, near the big rivers." He hesitated for a moment, then said, "Listen, can I ask you a question?"

"Shoot," said Ski.

"You just mentioned an orphanage a few miles north of here. What kind of an orphanage is it?"

"Just an orphanage," said Ski, "for kids with no parents, mainly because of the war. It's run by nuns left over from the French occupation. They didn't leave when they had the chance. They've been in charge of that place for a while, and they really care about those kids."

Britman could hear the passion in Ski's voice. "Sounds like you do too, Sir. Listen, can we meet later?" he asked. "I have something I need to do, and you guys might be able to help."

Terry looked at Ski, puzzled. Britman saw the expression and figured he needed to tell them a little more. "Look, you're going to an orphanage—you obviously care about kids." His voice grew urgent. "I'll get you a case of rations if you come and hear me out."

"What the heck?" said Ski. "A case of Lerps is worth a little conversation anytime? We'll take that.

By the way, what's your team name?"

"Angel," replied Britman.

"Doggone," said Ski. "I'm Aloft Three-Two and this is Aloft Three-Four. We've provided air cover for you guys lots of times. How's Gabriel?"

"The El Tee. is fine. I just spoke to him a little while ago. I guess we have a lot in common. It would be good to just compare notes. We never really get to meet any of our cover pilots—at least not face to face. Are we on for our meeting, Sir?"

"You bet! It'll be fun to meet the guys behind the voices."

It took Brit a few minutes to explain how to get to his company area and which hooch was his. When he was done, he shook hands with the two pilots, saluted, turned around—and amazingly, the line for the PX was gone.

"Four more," said the soldier standing at the PX door. Terry and Ski went into the building through the big metal doors.

* * *

Brit was already hurrying back to his hooch to talk to the others. They had to make a plan. Was this the answer for the kid? Could he really trust these two young pilots, or were they a couple of by-the-book assholes who'd turn him in? He was hoping that his prayers had been answered. He'd know tonight. His heart was racing.

* * *

At the ripe old age of six, he had seen a lot. His earliest memories were of moving from place to place with his mother and father. Sometimes they lived in villages. Sometimes they lived in little towns. His father had been teaching him how to speak French, and he'd been doing pretty well at it. It was a lot different than Vietnamese. He liked the way it sounded—softer. His parents spoke both languages, but mostly Vietnamese in public. In private, they spoke French.

But so much had happened in the last few weeks. He'd watched as the soldiers who spoke his native language had trapped his father and beat him up. He didn't know why. He just knew that when he and his mother had left the last plantation, they'd left without his father. He was told his father was gone. When he'd asked when he would be back, his mother cried and said he would not be coming back. He missed his father a lot. And now he was in strange place, with strange people he could not understand, and he didn't know where his mother was. The bump on his head hurt. He was getting fed, and that was good. And the people that were taking care of him were nice to him but . . . he just wanted to go back to his mother.

The boy was asleep and hidden on a bunk at the back of the room when the other men arrived at Sgt. Britman's hooch. The evening rain was falling in buckets when Terry and Ski knocked on the door. They both were pretty wet, but they were used to it. Brit welcomed them and looked around outside before he closed the door. He offered them a towel.

Doc was sitting on a bunk on one side of the small room. Brit introduced him. "This is Specialist Jacobson. We call him Doc." A couple of chairs were squeezed in between the bunks.

Doc stood up and shook Terry's hand, then Ski's. "So you're Lerp cover pilots? Brit says we've worked with you before. El Tee and our radio man, Zac, would probably know your voices right off. They're the ones who always make the calls to you."

Doc sat back down on the bunk. Brit motioned to the two chairs and sat down on the other bunk. Terry and Ski sat down.

Brit started talking about the AO they were currently working and some of what they faced moving through the jungle. He talked a bit about the beauty of the areas around the rivers and how fast the water flowed, especially after a legendary downpour like they were now experiencing. It was interesting to hear their perspective about life as a ground-pounder.

"Being on the ground you learn to be aware of every smell and every sound," said Britman. "There is a lot of things to see, interesting flowers I have never seen before. Some funny looking insects. But you worry which ones might be poisonous."

"Around the base here we just look out for the rats" said Terry.

"They're scarry enough for me" said Ski.

Brit started to roll his eyes but caught himself and said "you have no idea what it's like out there. I wish rats were all we had to worry about."

Then he changed the subject.

"So what do you think of our mission here?" he asked cautiously.

Terry sensed his caution. It was like he was testing them. "I'm not sure," he answered. "There are a lot of things I don't understand. Like, there is a lot of time where we know where the enemy is, but they won't let us attack. What's up with that?"

Brit answered shaking his head affirmatively, "I know what you mean. We can't get any firepower until we yell 'contact.'"

Can I trust these guy, Wondered Brit.

After about ten minutes of banter about the war, Terry sensed Brit was getting more serious. He thought to himself, *he is feeling us out. I wonder what that is all about..*

Then Brit abruptly changed the subject again. "Tell me," he said, "you guys have any kids?"

"Not me," said Terry as he looked at Ski. "I've only been married . . . well, less than a year. Not enough time. I'm not sure this is even the right time, ya know? I mean, I have a few issues right now, but kids would be nice someday."

Ski looked down at the floor, then back to Sgt. Britman. "Someday," he said. "Someday my wife and I hope to have a baby boy . . . maybe a couple of girls too." He smiled. "Why do you ask?"

"I just need to know if you like kids," said Brit.

Where is he going with this, Terry thought to himself.

Brit was no youngster. He was older than most of the men in his company, maybe the oldest. But the average age of a soldier serving in Vietnam was nineteen or twenty, so that wasn't saying much. Terry guessed Brit was in his early thirties. He was a seasoned NCO and no doubt knew his way around the military. Terry and Ski were just in their early twenties.

"Yes," said Ski. "I like children. I haven't seen many lately though, have you? I have seen a lot of very young adults that never had a chance to be children." He paused. "Except . . ."

"Except what?" Brit wanted to know.

"Except at the orphanage. The one I was talking about this afternoon. There are still some kids there that are getting a little bit of a childhood."

Doc shot a look at Brit. "Go for it," he said.

Brit nodded. "Sir, sorry I've been beating about the bush. I need some special help, and you're it. I guess I gotta trust that you're not sticklers for regs."

Ski and Terry looked at each other and they both laughed out loud. "Oh, you have nothing to worry about there. We seem to be very creative in finding new ways to break 'em."

Brit looked over at Doc and gave him a thumbs-up. Then Doc sat forward, moved a pillow from the front of his bunk, and pulled back the covers. Gently he reached down and picked up the young boy who'd been asleep under the bedroll and sat him on his lap. He was dressed in cut-down jungle fatigues that were still far too big for him. He was barefoot, and the bandage on the back of his head was visible. He rubbed his eyes and looked around, but didn't say a word.

They all sat quietly for a minute. Then Brit said, "You need to understand, he's special. We found him in the jungle. He'd been left for dead. You probably can't see from there, but he has blue eyes. He can't stay here with us. And if he goes out there"—Brit gestured in the general direction of the jungle—"the VC will more than likely kill him just because they can."

"So when you heard me mention the orphanage, you thought—"

"Yes, Sir. I thought maybe he would fit in there . . . be safe, you know? Can he?"

"How did you get him in here, past the gate guards and all?"

"Huey. Came back with us when we pulled out of our last mission, flew right into the compound. Nobody asked any questions. It's only the grouchy MPs at the front gate that ask questions."

Ski got up from his chair and sat down on the bunk next to Doc and the boy. "Can I hold him?"

Doc carefully shifted the boy from his lap to Ski's. Ski put his arms around him and held him close. The little boy looked up at Ski, then back at Doc. He wasn't sure what to do. Ski looked over at Brit. "We can't have kids, my wife and I," he admitted. "We'd give anything for a beautiful child like this."

Terry was astonished. Ski had never mentioned that before, but it explained a lot. "Can you get him out?" he said. "Can you get a helicopter and drop him off at the orphanage tomorrow, say about 0900? We'll make the arrangements."

"Can we do it Wednesday?" said Brit. "We're going back in for a ten-day, and we can drop him on the way. We have good chopper pilots that pretty much do what we ask."

"That works," said Ski. "We'll tell the nuns you're coming. And don't forget that case of rations. Drop it off at the same time."

The next day, Monday, Ski, Terry and Pop went to the orphanage as planned. They explained the situation to the nuns who willingly agreed to accept the boy into their care.

Two days later, Wednesday morning, Sister Ellen met the men from the helicopter. It landed in the clearing beyond the dead trees. There were two of them that came out of the side door of the Huey—Doc and Britman. "I was told you would be coming," she said to them.

The two soldiers holding the boy were dressed in jungle fatigues. They appraised her, then Doc said, "Please treat him well. And by the way, he doesn't say much, and we don't speak Vietnamese, so we've been getting by the best we can. Hope you have better luck."

"Are you sure he'll be safe here?" asked Britman.

Sister Louise came up behind the other nun just as Brit asked the question. "Safer than just about anywhere else around here," she said to Sister Ellen in French half under her breath and directed toward Sister Ellen.

The boy looked up, a smile on his face. He immediately started speaking in French and asked the sisters if they knew his mama.

The four of them stood there for a moment, stunned. The boy repeated his question, then launched into a conversation in French with the nuns.

"Guess we have something to share with the guys when we get back," said Doc.

"Yeah. We lucked out and found just the right place," Britman said.

Sister Ellen turned back to the two soldiers. "Thank you, gentlemen. We will take it from here. We'll find out what we can and let you know what happens."

The boy wiggled loose from Sister Louise, who'd been holding him. He ran over to Doc and hugged him on the leg. Britman crouched down and patted him on the head. The boy stood back, put his hands together and bowed, then turned and ran back to the nuns. Doc and Brit watched as the trio walked back to the compound, the boy holding a nun's hand in each of his own, all chattering in French.

Chapter 10

Because he knew his way around the military, and because he figured this was his last chance to add to his already considerable nest-egg, Pop had volunteered for Vietnam. His experience had taught him that there was no better place for a creative entrepreneur to make a substantial amount of off-the-record income than in the tangled morass of a war zone.

Before he'd left the states, he'd put in place a secret money machine. Only Pop and his dear and trusted friend back in Hawaii knew how all the pieces came together. That way no one person could cut him out. He knew that the military put restrictions in place to keep soldiers from profiting from their service in combat. It was just another thing that made no sense. Of course, it never occurred to most soldiers to do anything for profit while doing their duty, but old timers remembered what things were like in past wars.

One of the things the government tried to do was keep US dollars from becoming currency among the locals and hence be used against them. When new soldiers came into the country, they had a three-day wait period before assignment to their post. Generally they were assigned to a replacement company like the Ninetieth Repo Depot. One of the things that happened when they arrived was that they were ordered to exchange any American currency they had for MPCs—Military Payment Certificates—which were issued dollar for dollar for the greenbacks. The difference was, it was colored various other colors—red, blue, yellow, but never green. It was also different sizes. The ten was the biggest, the five slightly smaller, and the one smaller still.

There was also paper currency for what would normally be coins, all in descending sizes. They had different pictures and symbols on them, and soldiers often puzzled over the imagery.

The difficulty this presented to Pop and others like him was that it was a challenge to move any profits earned in 'Nam back to the US. The MPC was worthless stateside, and a soldier was only allowed to convert $2,000 back to greenbacks on his departure back to the states.

For Pop, who had carefully planned his operation, this created just another profit opportunity. He set up a network of field agents who could arrange for sums of money that exceeded the limit to be transferred into the US, but there was always a percentage and a surcharge. Pop chose his agents carefully and cut them in on the profits. It was kept in the shadows and spoken only as "I know someone who knows someone who may be able to help you." Pop worked hard to minimize the risk of getting caught.

One captain named Ralph Horse, also a pilot, had hooked up with Pop early on. They were in the same RAC unit. He was the best poker player around and consistently made $10,000 or more a month in winnings. Pop set him up so that his money got back home every couple of months, just like clockwork.

This part of the money thing was Pop's plan "B." There was also plan "C" and others, but plan "A" was the cash cow. It took nearly a year to set up, and with the help of his former B-29 commander, Captain Roger McGreggor, it would leave both of them well-off for life. Once a month, Pop and Roger performed a major money exchange.

* * *

Roger's B-29 had taken some flak during a raid over Tokyo, and it nearly cost him his right leg. The crew made it back, thanks to a good copilot and a sturdy airplane. Pop had crawled out of his gun position in the tail and made it up to the front, and he'd helped pull Roger out of the pilot's seat. He helped to bandage the leg, stop the bleeding, and did what he could to stabilize it.

The copilot had switched over to the captains seat on the left. Pop, ever the adventurer, had been a rookie barnstormer and was a pretty good pilot. He climbed up into the right seat. He didn't attempt to fly the big bomber—he just wanted to relieve the work load and help the copilot by assuming some of his former responsibilities so he could concentrate on flying.

When they got back to base and the doctors took over, they did all they could to put Roger's leg back together, but there was so much damage to the muscle and the bone that they had no choice but to cut it off just above the knee. He'd been a great pilot who'd wanted to work in the budding field of commercial aviation and join one of the new airlines that were springing up. But that dream was shattered along with his leg in a single bright AA burst near the nose of his B-29.

Roger was transferred to the new Tripler Army Hospital in Hawaii. While he was recuperating, he was able to get a feel for the island life, and it just seemed to set well with him. After he was discharged, he decided to stay in Hawaii. There wasn't much left for him stateside. His sullen and bitter mood, as expressed in his letters home, had led to a breakup with his childhood sweetheart. He really didn't want to go back with one leg. And now where was he? Sure, he got his benefits, medical and military disability, but it wasn't what he had planned for his life.

By the time Pop Danforth showed up, Roger had become rather withdrawn. It was over a year since the end of the war, and nearly two years since he'd lost his leg. He'd rented a small apartment not far from the beach, and pretty much just stayed to himself.

Pop had done a bit of research just to find him. Not much stopped Pop—and there he was, standing outside an oceanfront apartment on a beautiful day within sight of Diamond Head on the island of Oahu, knocking on the red front door of Captain Roger (Stick) McGreggor.

Pop was always a mystery. No one ever really knew what was going on inside his head. But he had certain qualities that those who knew him best understood and appreciated. For one, he was fiercely loyal to his true friends—and, two, he could always be counted on for a plan.

The door opened. "Danforth—what the hell are you doing here?" said Roger, surprised.

"Hey, Stick. I was in the neighborhood and I thought I'd drop by." Not exactly truthful, since he'd caught a hop and flown in on a cargo plane a couple of hours ago, just to find his old friend.

"So are you gonna tell me how you found me, Danny?" asked Roger, still standing at the open door.

Without missing a beat, Pop said, "I'm a Jehovah's Witness, just out knocking on doors. Hell, what a surprise. As long as I'm here, I figure you may need me to stay and straighten you out. You going to invite me in, or should I just leave one of my brochures?"

Roger smiled and opened the door, motioning for Danny to come in. He was a bit thinner. He was only about five years older than Danforth, and he'd always been slender, but now he looked gaunt. Danforth could see the quick eyes of the pilot that had gotten him through a tough bombing run on more than one occasion. What was missing was the fire and determination. He saw it as perhaps the loss of . . . vision—not the kind that you have in your eyes, the kind you have in your heart when you have a plan for the future. It was just a gut feeling, and his gut was seldom wrong. And as he glanced around the room, he could see the clutter and the spent bottles of beer and vodka. It occurred to him that maybe that was why he was looking so thin.

Stick went to the refrigerator. It was a small one with a single door on four six-inch porcelain-clad legs, and there was a round metal coil on the top. It seemed pretty fancy on Stick's income. He pulled out two bottles of cold beer and handed one to Danforth. "Come on out here," he said as he motioned to the small patio that faced the ocean. They sat down on two bamboo chairs facing the surf, the sound of the waves filling their ears.

That was the continuation of an amazing journey, and the beginning of a lifelong partnership. They decided to go into business together. Danny, as Stick called him, had saved some money, and with Stick's retirement income, they bought a small pawn shop across from Waikiki Beach, on Honolulu's main drive. Stick became the face of the business and a prominent member of the community. He joined the Lions Club and was known for his generosity and community projects. He met a lot of other officers and former officers, and developed ongoing relationships with them. Pop and Stick brought them all together and the ones who caught the vision, they formed an investment group. In 1950 they bought out a small savings and loan just up the street from the pawn shop. Stick became the president of the bank, and he hired another of his trustworthy fellow officers to look after the pawn shop. It was all part of the long-range plan that Danny had put in place.

When the Korean "Police Action" began, Danny went back into the army—with the rank of staff sergeant, because of his prior service. This was where the next pieces of the puzzle would come into play. Danny became a supply sergeant, and because of his talents, he soon became the go-to guy for people who needed things that they couldn't get through normal channels. It was also the first time he'd be able to try out his plan to use what had been called Allied Military Currency during WWII, to begin to amass his fortune. For the Korean War, the name of the currency was changed Military Payment Certificates, but the concept was the same.

When Vietnam got going, he found an even more screwed-up conflict than Korea. Vietnam was full of strange opportunities. The base clubs had acquired slot machines, for instance.

They took tokens that were handled by the bartender. It seemed out of character for the military, but he never questioned it. Because he was naturally curios, he watched to see what might happen. But he wasn't going to rock the boat because he had his own business going on, and if he called attention to one, it might call attention to his.

The MPC exchange was more efficient in Vietnam, but it still had its holes—and unless you were someone who'd been planning for just such an event for the last fifteen years, they weren't easy to find. Pop wasn't an educated man, but in his own way, he was a genius.

Chapter 11

"Supply is missing four parachutes. Do you know anything about that, Mr. Danforth?" said the CO in a commanding voice.

Warrant Officer Danforth was standing at attention before the company commander of the Eighty-ninth RAC, Major Pratt. The XO was standing beside the major, who was seated behind the desk. It was a small office with just enough room for a desk and a couple of chairs. Against the wall was a gray metal filing cabinet with a thermite grenade strapped to the top. In case the enemy overran the base, the nearest person would pull the pin, and the grenade, mainly white phosphorous, would melt through the filing cabinet, destroying all the documents on its way to the bottom. Once ignited, there was virtually no way of putting it out.

"Listen to me, Pop," said the CO, using Danforth's more familiar nickname. "I'm signed for everything in this company, and when I leave, you make damn sure everything I signed for is present and accounted for. Understand?"

"Yes, Sir," answered Pop. The CO knew that Warrant Officer Danforth was probably the oldest guy in the company. The first sergeant was in his mid forties, but Pop was older. Pratt knew he'd been in the military for a lifetime, and that Pop knew the ins and outs just by virtue of his vast experiences. He was a legend because of his exploits during WWII, when he'd been a tail gunner on a B-29 that had bombed the site where the RAC Company was now situated. It was common knowledge that it was a Japanese airfield back then. Now it was a US Army airfield located near the village of Phu Loi. Having been in and out of the military system ever since his tail gunner days, he'd somehow gotten the army to send him through the Warrant Officer Candidate Flight School Program—further embellishing his legend. He'd graduated as a "Wobbly One"—Warrant Officer First Class. In Vietnam he acted a little unorthodox most of the time. He didn't wear a regulation army hat. Instead he had a ten-gallon cowboy hat that looked like it had been swiped from Hoss Cartright. On the front of the hat was a pair of army aviator wings, a pair of US Air Force crew member wings, and a pair of glider pilot wings. They were all pinned on the hat—one above the other, and all above his current rank insignia, which was now W.II. Atop his tall slender frame, the hat looked strange, to say the least. But that was just Pop.

One of Danforth's extra duties was supply chief. It was his job to see to it that everything listed in the company TO&E were present and accounted for. Things that were consumables had to be used in reasonable amounts, and the paperwork had to reflect their status accurately.

"Sir, I'm not sure, but I think I can find those parachutes," said Pop confidently. "I think what may have happened is that the last supply guy sent some of them out for their repacking cycle, and we just didn't get 'em all back." What he didn't say was that he'd taken the parachutes and traded them for something else that he or one of his friends needed. He was already working on a way to replace them. He was surprised that his little misappropriation had been discovered so quickly. What few people knew was that Pop was a major scrounge, and even fewer knew of his greater strategy. He had a network of people and favors that he'd developed over many years. A war zone was the perfect place to magnify his talents. So many things happened there that could be written off to consumption, battle damage, or local theft. Pop was working those deals to put together the finishing touches on his retirement nest-egg. Only he knew all the details.

For some reason, he took a liking to Terry. "I'm gonna show you how to make things happen around here," he'd tell him. It was as if he'd found a student recruit to pass on all his information to, and he liked that. And when they'd take a walk somewhere private, like out on the flight line, he'd explain how to get around regular army channels. Pop's quarters had an air-conditioner, and before long, with Pop's tutelage, so did Terry's. Only a couple of rooms had A/C, and to Terry and his roommates, it made a huge difference in the quality of their sleep. Pop had bartered for his A/C with a parachute, although not any of the missing ones. He'd gotten this parachute by trading some Lerp rations for a special favor.

It was a little different for Terry. His roommate had gotten his air conditioner out of a burned-out storage container. When Terry first got there, it wasn't working consistently. He was told it needed a part—a capacitor. Pop told him where to get it, and they'd bluffed their way into the reclamation center to look around. They found an old ice machine just sitting out in the dirt. The sergeant who ran the place wasn't about to give up anything, even if it was useless to him. So while Pop and Terry distracted his attention on other matters, Spec Four Pulaski, who'd come along with them just for something to do, took a pair of wire clippers, removed it from the ice machine, and put it in his pocket. It was only the size of a roll of half dollars, so it was easy to conceal. When they got back to their quarters, Terry took the air conditioner apart and replaced the old metal canister with the new one. That did the trick. It worked pretty well after that. As long as the generator was putting out full power, there was no problem. But when the power was weak, the air conditioner compressor had a hard time starting. When his roommate left, he sold the A/C unit to Terry for $500. He would have charged him $1,000, but he figured Terry had a part in making it work, so he deserved a discount.

Recon Airplane Company: III Corps, Vietnam

On their days off, Pop and Terry would take one of the company airplanes and fly around to different bases and make friends with various people. Pop always carried a little bartering material, and often let his trading partners get the better end of the trade. He also had a small spiral-bound notebook that he carried in his upper shirt pocket. His notebook was his reminder. So he always remembered who they were, where they were, what they had, and what they wanted. Some guys had connections for stuff that they brought back from R&R in Thailand or Hong Kong. Other guys had access to special food, like steaks, which Pop regularly acquired by the case. Enemy rifles and ordnance were always in demand. Pop ran the operation like an in-house black market. He even used the real in-country black market in Saigon to get some of the things he wanted. He once traded two air-conditioners and some other unspoken special favors for an army OV-1 Mohawk twin engine prop jet aircraft worth several million dollars—that is, if you could even buy one. Seems it had been rebuilt out of crashed planes and spare parts, and it wasn't on any inventory list. The guys who had it were leaving the country and couldn't make a deal with anyone for it. But they could sell the two air conditioners for over a thousand bucks each. To them, it was better than nothing. To Pop, it was the ultimate deal—it was always about the deal. Now where was he going to park it? Pop had plans for that plane. He just had to have the right opportunity for it to pay off.

Some of their trading trips resulted in the best times they ever had—like when they went to Phan Rang to buy lobsters. A party was planned for the XO, who was being promoted to major. He commissioned Pop, his chief scrounge, to get the best fixings he could. Pop made up a menu and accessory list and went to work. He assigned Terry the task of going to Phan Rang for lobster.

Terry flew the Beaver to Phan Rang. Ski went along for the ride, and this time he flew in the copilot's seat. The little seaport village had almost no room for a runway so a PSP (perforated steel planking) runway had been constructed on the beach—sheets of steel with round holes that hooked together to achieve the required length. The wind was blowing hard from the ocean, which created a direct crosswind to the strip. Terry had to dip the wing almost to the runway to get the plane on the ground and keep it going in the right direction. He got it down, taxied back, and with the help of his crew chief, tied it down near the makeshift control tower.

The airfield tower chief let them borrow his Jeep to go into town. It was about a five-minute drive and the ocean breeze felt nice. It was cooler on the coast near the ocean than it was inland. The breeze from the ocean was a refreshing change. The village was made up of mostly fishermen and their families. There was a central marketplace with rows of vendors selling their goods. There were vegetables, clothing, and lots of freshly caught fish. They walked around, trying to find lobster. They found the prize toward the end of one row of fish vendors. It wasn't what they had expected. They were not the live lobsters found in a stateside fish market. These were just tails, and they thought they were somewhat smaller than they should be. Terry tried to explain that they wanted bigger ones, but the vendor said these were all they had. Terry paid for them in the local currency of piasters, and in his head quickly calculated the cost at about twenty cents a pound. Even if they were a little small, it was a good deal. They took all they could find from two different venders, winding up with two full cases. Pop would be pleased that his training had paid off so well.

As they wandered around the village and the market, they remarked to each other that the people seemed different here. They were self sufficient, they didn't need their government to supply their food. They didn't need outsiders telling them how to live. They were living off the land and sea, just as their ancestors had done for centuries. Although the vendors shrank back a little when Terry and Ski stopped to talk to them, they didn't seem intimidated. So many villagers they encountered in the interior wouldn't even come near them. These people even smiled sometimes. Children ran through the streets, playing their games. For those few hours, it seemed that they'd stepped out of the war zone and into the real world. To Terry it felt good.

When they got back to Phu Loi and unloaded their precious cargo, Pop was there to meet them. He took one case of the lobster, threw it into the back of his Jeep, and disappeared. He was back a couple hours later with a case of filet mignon that he'd traded for the lobster.

That evening, all the pilots not on duty gathered in the Officers' Club. Outside, the barbecue was cooking steaks and lobster. Inside, the beer and champagne were abundant. It turned out to be the best promotion party the company ever had. Maj. Randolph got wasted and ate a couple of bites out of his glass just to prove his manhood. Capt. MacDillard got mad at one of the guys he was playing poker with and shot another hole in the ceiling with his .45. Terry left early for a Lerp mission. He ate a steak—medium rare, just how he liked it—and some potato salad. He never did care for lobster. As he was leaving, he saw Pop in the corner with somebody from Battalion HQ, whom he had invited. They seemed to be close to a deal on something. Maybe they could get that stupid OV-1 Mohawk off the flight line. Nobody in the company was checked out on it anyway.

* * *

As Terry was climbing up to altitude in his Bird Dog, the air grew a little cooler. Flying at night was always refreshing. The air was calm, and the drone of the engine made the world feel a bit more peaceful. He opened the side windows, rolled up his sleeves, and rested his elbows on the window frame. He took a deep breath of the fresh night air. The lights of Saigon were on the horizon. He thought to himself, *This is where I belong—up here in the sky*. He didn't mean Vietnam. In many ways, he was living a dream—his dream. By now he had a few hundred flying hours, and he knew that by the time he left 'Nam, he'd have over a thousand. It was a great start on the experience required to apply with an airline. *Where will it take me?* he mused. He tuned the ADF radio to AFVN and listened for a little while. Not much on, and the music wasn't his style. He turned it off and went back to his thoughts. What does a soldier think about in a war zone when he has time to think? He had that luxury sometimes—especially on night flights.

His thoughts wandered. *What about this war? We don't get much information from home.* He wouldn't learn that the antiwar protests had escalated until he returned home, and he was unaware of the growing sentiment against returning vets. There had been some protests when he was in college in '66, and there had been some discussion about the country's involvement. But he'd been insulated while at basic training, advanced individual training, OCS, and flight school. For those two years, he'd heard the news the army way. He was preparing to do his duty for his country, as generations before him had. He was surrounded by those ready to do the same.

Terry thought that a lot of his feelings came from growing up in a small town, from some of the great teachers he had in school. In those days, they studied the constitution and the founding fathers. He was proud of his country and its origins, how the colonists fought for independence and individual freedom. The historic documents—the Declaration of Independence, the Preamble to the Constitution, the Gettysburg Address—said it so clearly. That was what this war was all about to him—to give these people the same opportunities in life that were his at birth. And that was a hard thing to grasp at times, when he saw how they chose to live. They were people who built ramps out into the Saigon River so they could shit in the same water that others downstream had to drink. The same people who threw their children in front of army Jeeps so they could make a claim against the US government. Their lives, their customs, their culture wasn't wrong—just very different from his idea of normal.

But the optimist in him thought he might be able to help make it better. *That's why I'm here, isn't it?* he thought. *We just have to get the goddamn communists off their backs.*

He knew there were others who had different reasons for being there. The lifers had a saying: "It's not much of a war, but it's the only war we got." A lot of them were just looking for the combat experience to help them with promotions. A lot of them probably didn't think about the consequences, just the self-serving aspects. Some guys were gung ho and loved the battles and the body count. But Terry liked to think that most were like him—a little skeptical, a lot patriotic, just doing what their leaders told them what was best for their country and the little nation of South Vietnam. They were all just doing their duty.

His reflections were interrupted when his primary radio come to life. "Aloft, Aloft," came the hushed voice over the Bird Dog's radio. "This is Angel Bravo."

Terry had only been on station for about thirty minutes and was just switching fuel tanks from left wing to right wing. His thumb moved up to the mike switch on the control stick. "Angel Bravo, this is Aloft, go ahead."

"Aloft, we've got a problem. Please relay a message back to HQ, over."

"Sure—ready to copy." Terry took his grease pencil and prepared to write on the Plexiglas window on the right side of the cockpit.

"We have a medical emergency down here and we need a medivac as soon as we can get it, over." That was easy enough. No need to write that down.

"Okay—let me see what I can do. Break. Oxide Vapor base, this is Aloft Three-Four, over."

There was a short silence, and Terry took the time to orient the Bird Dog in the direction of team Angel Bravo. Then he tried again. "Oxide Vapor base, this is Aloft Three-Four, over."

"Aloft Three-Four, Oxide Vapor base, go ahead."

"Snake Base, Team Bravo is reporting a medical emergency and requesting an ASAP medevac, over."

"Okay—stand by."

The lush green jungle slid below the wings of the Bird Dog. Flying at about 4,000 feet, Terry could keep radio contact with all the teams in the AO and relay their radio transmissions back to base camp. There were five teams out there today. A few miles ahead, he could see where the rivers Song Be and Dong Nai came rushing together, and farther north the checkpoint the pilots called the Big Bend.

There were no roads to be seen, only jungle and clearing, and sometimes an area of large bomb craters created by a past B-52 Arc Light strike, otherwise known as carpet bombing.

As he approached the area where team Bravo was last reported, the radio came to life again. "Aloft Three-Four, Oxide Vapor base. Say the nature of the emergency."

"This is Aloft . . . they said it's medical."

"We need a specific, Aloft. Ask 'em what's going on." came the rather curt reply.

"Stand by. Break. Bravo, this is Aloft. Say the nature of the medical emergency."

It took a little longer than usual for the team to respond. Terry was about to key his mike again and repeat the call when the answer came.

"Hang on Aloft—Gabriel wants to talk to you."

The platoon leader? That's odd, thought Terry. Then a new voice came over the radio.

"Aloft, this is Gabe. We have a situation. One of my troops has the clap. He didn't know it, he got out here, and now he can't whiz. His pecker's turning purple, and he's in a lot of pain. Oh yeah, he's also turning yellow in the eyes and skin. Doc says he has to have treatment soon."

"Man alive, Gabe, I'll see what they say," said Terry, picking up on the concern in the platoon leader's voice. "Oxide Vapor base, this is Aloft." Terry relayed the situation back to base camp.

"Okay Aloft. Got it. Stand by." In a few moments, Oxide Vapor came back on the radio. "Aloft, relay to Bravo. Scheduled extraction in four days as planned."

"Oxide Vapor, are you serious?" said Terry incredulously.

"That comes right from Six, Aloft. Relay it!" the operator said, more like an order than a request. In the military, numbers in call signs mean something. Five is the executive officer. Six is the CO. One through four are the numbers of various staff members..

He wasn't pleased to have to relay the new order. "Bravo, this is Aloft Three-Four—Oxide Vapor Six says four days till extraction, as per schedule."

"Aloft, this is Gabe, I'll get back to you."

Terry could hear the irritation in the platoon leader's voice. He wouldn't have asked for the medevac if he didn't think he really needed it.

Terry had seen the training films. Hell, he'd even taught some of the classes when he was back at Fort Benning as a basic training officer. They were given to all army personnel. They detailed how you could get syphilis, gonorrhea, and a host of other sexual transmitted diseases. They showed what to do to prevent infection. And they showed the consequences of not being treated in a timely fashion. This soldier could die, although that was unlikely. But he probably would end up with some serious problems with his liver or bladder, and there was a real chance that he would end up sterile. And right now he was in pain—maybe worse pain than enemy torture.

"Aloft, this is Gabe. Call back and see if you can talk to Six directly. I need to know why we can't get this kid out of here."

"Okay, I'll see what I can do. By the way, how old is this kid?"

"Seventeen, why?"

"Just curious."

Terry could tell that Gabe was furious, and he was a little upset as well. What could this CO be thinking?

"Oxide Vapor base, this is Aloft."

"Go ahead, Aloft."

"Can you put Six on the horn?"

"Hang on, I'll ask."

Terry could just picture some major sitting in the Tactical Operations Center, giving orders and listening to the radio. He'd be surprised if he picked up the mike.

"Aloft, Six says he's listening, go ahead."

Just as he thought—Commanding Officer Jerk. "Sir, this is Aloft Three-Four. Gabe respectfully asks why he can't have the medevac now."

Pause.

"Six says the mission calls for a seven-day insertion, and that's what it will be—wait a second, hang on, Aloft—"

A new voice came on the radio, with defiant authority. "Aloft, this is Six. You tell Gabe his troop made a big mistake, and he's just going to have to live with it."

Terry was continuing to circle his Bird Dog in the general vicinity of the Lerp team. "Sir, please consider that this kid is only seventeen. It's probably his first time away from home, and at seventeen, we both know he's a volunteer."

"Aloft, listen to me, do not—I repeat, do not—get in the middle of this, do you understand me?"

"Yes sir, break. Bravo, this is Aloft."

"Go ahead, Aloft."

"The CO says your troop made a big mistake, it's not his problem, and the kid will just have to live with it until the scheduled end of the mission."

"You're shitting me?"

"Sorry," said Terry as he made another adjustment to his throttle.

"Crap. I heard your plug. Thanks for trying."

Terry was frustrated. These troops on the ground were his responsibility too. He'd spent a lot of time flying cover for them. He'd called in gunships when they made enemy contact. He'd found them when they'd gotten lost. All the Aloft pilots looked after their teams like mother hens looks after their chicks. It probably wasn't right, but it was worth a try.

"Six, this is Aloft."

"What now. Aloft?" came the quick, blunt reply.

"Sir, when I was in OCS, they taught us the value of our men, and this guy is hurting and he's a detriment to the team and the mission. He may deserve an Article 15, but I don't think he or his team deserve this."

"Aloft? What's your call sign?"

"Aloft Three-Four, Sir."

"You've crossed the line, Son. I learned my lessons at West Point, and I'm not about to have some OCS junior officer tell me how to run my battalion."

Battalion? Shit. He's probably a Lt. Colonel, or maybe even a full bull, thought Terry.

"Now get back to your job, Aloft! The subject is closed."

"Yes Sir, Aloft out," Terry said crisply. He felt a range of emotions. He was intimidated by the superior officer; after all, he was a mere captain. But he was also angry at what he thought was a serious error in judgment. But what could he do about it? He could relay the story to his own superiors, but that could cause problems as well. As it was, he would probably get some kind of reprimand through official channels.

"Aloft, this is Gabe. I heard you trying. Thanks—we'll do what we can here, no need to reply."

"Roger," was all Terry could say, although a plan was formulating in his head. There had to be a way around that SOB commander. Pop had taught him that there was always a way around the stupid bureaucracy. Always. You just had to find it.

Terry went off shift at 1100 hours, and wasn't due back on until noon the next day. When he got back to the hooch he asked his section leader, Mike, to take a walk with him over to the Class VI store to pick up some scotch. On the way, he told him the story. Mike listened and shook his head. "You don't know the whole story, Terry. There may be more to it . . . on both sides. But I understand how you feel."

Terry just shook his head. "I know Gabe, sort of. I've met his team. He's a good guy. Sensible guy. No army BS. And he's there in the field. The colonel's not. The colonel should trust the judgment of his officers Hell, they don't even think about spending a million bucks for a B52 strike against a non-existant enemy base camp, but they won't shorten a mission by a couple of days to save the future of one of our own."

"You think there's something you can do about it?" said Mike.

"No—and it frustrates the hell outta me. Shit. I'm gonna get some chow and take a nap. Thanks for listening."

* * *

What Terry was discovering was that there is always a way around the military regulations and around idiotic commanders. He just had to work on a plan.

In the mean time, another plan was developing. Ski had already started the paper work to try to adopt the orphan boy that had been found in the jungle. But like any good planner, he knew he would have to have options. Who better to help figure this out than Pop?

No one else was in the little officers club at that early morning. They had all the privacy they needed to discuss ideas.

"You know what Ski?" said Pop. "I think I may have a way to do this but it is going to take a bit of work. We may need to pull in a couple other guys to help us. Whatever we do, it must be super secret. The less that the guys know about it, the better."

"Who do you suggest" said Ski.

"Let me think about that. I'll let you know. In the meantime I need your word that what I share with you is between us only. Got it?"

Ski nodded yes and caught the sparkle in Pop's eye.

Pop felt that surge of adrenalin that he always got when he was going after something that was a new adventure. This one had a little more danger than usual.

"This is my plan" said Pop.

* * *

Down in the jungle, team Angel Bravo was doing what they were trained to do—listen for enemy activity. It was dawn, and they had settled into their makeshift defense perimeter. It wasn't much—just some downed trees and a few leaves to conceal their location. The platoon doc was giving the disabled GI another shot of morphine, to see if he could get him to sleep without making any noise that would give away their position. Gabe was formulating a plan.

He knew what it would take to get an early medevac, and he planned to take action. He had to do it in such a way that involved no one else. That way, he'd be the only one to blame—and maybe he could pull it off without anyone suspecting. *Just another army bullshit thing*, he thought. Orders be damned. He was going to take care of his man. The man he'd trusted with his life wouldn't be left hanging out to dry if he could do anything about it.

* * *

Terry came back on shift the following day at 1200 hours. After he had taken his position reports from the other aircraft and heard it land back at base, he got on the radio and called the Angel Bravo team.

The RTO answered with a whisper. "Aloft, this is Angel, go ahead."

"Anything new?" Terry said.

There was a long pause as the RTO handed the mike and headphones off to his team leader. "Aloft, this is Gabe. From where we are, Oxide Vapor Control can't hear us. We've tried for the past couple of hours to call them direct just to make sure, and they don't answer. That is what we want right now."

"That's what I'm up here for, right?"

"Please listen and answer in short answers. We don't want this overheard by base."

"Roger that."

"This is Terry, right?" Terry thought it was curious that he would call him by name.

"Roger that," he answered, keeping it brief.

"Okay. My point man, Brit, says he knows you and you're helping out on another project involving a young boy and an orphanage. Don't answer that. He says I can trust you."

"Roger that."

"I want to say thanks a lot for trying to help last night. You put your ass on the line for us and we all appreciate it. I have a big favor to ask."

"Go ahead."

"You're going to figure this out in short order. I'm asking that you just follow my lead and give me all the help you can."

"Roger that."

Back at Oxide Vapor base, they were hearing Terry's rogers, but nothing from the team on the ground. They were getting curious. They radioed Terry. "Aloft Three-Four. Who are you talking to and what is it about?"

Terry really had no idea what was going on down on the ground, but he thought it must have something to do with the guy with the clap. He thought they must have some sort of plan, but he had no idea what it was. He decided to cover it the best he could.

"Oxide Vapor base, this is Aloft Three-Four. I was just talking to team Angel, and they were updating their position report."

"Roger," came the reply. "Carry on."

Gabe came back on. "I know you haven't figured this out yet, but thanks for the cover in the meantime. I'll be calling you back. Out."

Boy, there were a lot of questions there that needed an answer but there would be no way to ask without blowing up what was going on, whatever that was. It would be best to just conduct business as usual and wait for the next call.

While he waited for more information, Terry took the time to do an accurate locate on team Bravo by asking them to give him a "shiny." That meant that they should flash a mirror toward the airplane as it flew over. It wouldn't be seen on the ground, but it was a great way to spot the otherwise invisible team from the air.

Terry opened his map and looked at the terrain features. He used a grease pencil to mark the location of the team. "Bravo, I have you at Coors plus three, right four point two, copy?"

"Roger, Aloft. Can you spot a good LZ close by?" Terry banked the aircraft hard right and looked down searching for a suitable helicopter landing zone.

"Gimme a minute. Okay . . . yes. Try this one. Budweiser plus two, right two.

"Thanks, Aloft. This guy can hardly move. We're having to help him get around. One or two klicks is about all we can do."

Terry understood. One or two kilometers, klicks for short. Well, the LZ looked good enough for several choppers, so a medevac and a gunship should do just fine.

So as not to call too much suspicion about his activities, he decided to do a checkup on the rest of the AO. He started calling the other teams for updates. One requested a shiny for pinning down their location. Marching stealthily through jungles and then popping out in a clearing was sometimes disorienting, and the teams wanted to get an accurate position fix. The flashing mirror was the best way to pinpoint the team. He would then locate them from the air, pinpoint their position, and give them their map coordinates by using a special code like he'd used for Angel Bravo. It took about an hour to get all the teams double-checked.

And then it happened.

"Aloft, Aloft, this is Angel Bravo. Contact, repeat, contact." This time it was not the usual whisper, but a shout.

Terry's reaction was immediate. He made a tight turn and pointed the nose of the airplane at Angel Bravo's last known location. He pushed the throttle forward and listened as the 245-horsepower motor revved up to speed. The Bird Dog would only do ninety-five knots, but it was faster then the seventy he'd been doing a minute ago.

Contact was the magic word that meant they were under enemy fire.

As he was turning, he pushed the mike button forward with his thumb and called Vapor Control. "Oxide Vapor Control, this is Aloft Three-Four, Team Bravo reports contact."

Almost immediately control called back. "See if you can get azimuth and distance and send us the best known location for Angel Bravo."

Terry relayed the message. "Angel, can you give me contact azimuth and distance?"

It took almost a minute for the response, and when it came, Terry could hear automatic gunfire in the background. "Aloft, this is Angel. Three-two-zero degrees, sixty meters, do you copy?"

"Got it," Terry replied, "Three-two-zero at sixty." Then, "Oxide Vapor, this is Aloft Three-Two."

"Go ahead, Aloft," came the reply. "We copy three-two-zero degrees at sixty meters, correct?" They'd heard his transmission on the read-back to the team on the ground.

"Correct," answered Terry, "and their current location is"—he looked at his map to make sure—"from Budweiser, plus four . . . right seven point two. Copy?"

"Copy, from Budweiser, plus four . . . right seven point two. Got it. How big is the force?"

Terry called the team. " Bravo, please estimate size of force."

There was another pause. It seemed to take forever. Then, "Aloft, this is Bravo. We have more action at two-one-zero degrees. Numerous AK-47s and about two or three carbines. Looks like we may have moved into an ambush. Maybe twenty to thirty VC. We need help, now." This time he did not hear weapons fire in the background. It seemed odd.

"Roger Bravo. Break, Break. Oxide Vapor, more movement at two-one-zero and the estimate twenty to thirty VC with AK-47 and carbine. Requesting immediate help."

"Aloft, tell 'em we have already scrambled a flight of two Cobras and they're on the way."

Terry wasn't sure how much time that would take, so he decided to do a little checking on his own. He switched up the UHF radio that all US aircraft monitor when they're in flight and switched to transmit on 243.0, the international emergency frequency.

"Any combat-ready aircraft in the vicinity of the Song Be and Dong Nay rivers, this is Aloft Three-Four, we have troops in contact. Please respond if you can help and tell me what you have on board."

He switched to his FM radio and called Angel. "Angel, Oxide Vapor says they have Cobras scrambled. I'm trying to find other help as well. Do the best you can. The cavalry is on the way."

The reply was almost immediate. "Keep it coming, Aloft. We're in serious trouble." Once again he didn't hear any activity in the background. He was beginning to figure out the truth.

At the same time they were calling back to the Bird Dog, Terry's UHF radio came alive. "Aloft," came a calm voice. "This is Spooky Four-Four. I'm about five minutes away with a pair of gyro-mounted Vulcans. Can I help?"

"Perfect. Pick up a station over the junction of the rivers. They're not far from there. I'll guide you in when I have a hard fix on enemy locations."

The radio came alive again, this time on the team FM frequency. "Aloft, this is Snake One-Two and Snake One–Three, your Cobras. We're just coming off Bien Hoa and should be on station in about fifteen to twenty minutes."

"Great," said Terry. "I need to work you on a different frequency. Lets use 38.9 Fox Mike. Give me a call." Terry reached into the empty back seat and dialed up the observer's FM radio to 38.9. His adrenaline was kicking in, and all his training was coming into play. The Snakes were on frequency and waiting for the call. Now he had three radios in play. The base and team radio, the UHF for the Spooky, and the second FM for the Cobras.

Oxide Vapor came back on the radio. "What's happening up there, Aloft?" came the HQ controller in a calm, paced voice.

The controller's calm voice amazed him. Terry could not understand how someone could be so calm and dispassionate when they were sitting in the safety of their bunker and someone else's life was in imminent danger.

What Terry couldn't see was all the activity back in control. From the very moment Terry relayed the call of "contact," the entire room came to life. When the radio operator heard the word, even before he answered Terry's call, he shouted out "contact," and everyone in the TOC directed their attention to the matter at hand. The runner was given a slip of paper, and he ran out the door to find the commander, who was in the mess hall having lunch. Another man, a Spec Four, was quickly on the phone, trying to get through to the standby helicopter gunship team. The team ran to their ships and began getting ready for take off. One person stepped over to the "big board," the map of the AO, picked up a grease pencil, and started preparing to draw arrows to depict the action as they understood it.

That was when the radio operator had called Terry and asked for more information.

As Terry continued to relay the bits and pieces of information given to him by the combatants on the ground, the people in the TOC were breaking it down and trying to make sense of it all. Usually, when there was a ground firefight, the Lerps' commanding officer would jump into a Command and Control (C&C) ship like a Huey and fly to the scene. For some reason, today he chose not to do that, but decided to remain in the TOC and control the action from there.

Vapor Six, a full-bird colonel, came into the TOC, wiping lunch off his chin. "At ease," said the sergeant at the door, and everyone stood up.

"As you were," said Six in a practiced command voice. They all went back to what they were doing. "What's the situation?" he said sharply.

"Well, Sir," said the sergeant by the big board, "Angel Bravo is in contact at this time. The enemy is located here"—he pointed to the map—"and here. Charlie seems to be kind of in a semi-circle on the west side of the team in kind of a classic ambush maneuver."

"The guns were scrambled about five minutes ago and I think we are just confirming them airborne."

"How big a force do you think we're dealing with?" said Six as he walked toward the map.

"Well, they're estimating eight to ten here and . . . six or eight over here, and just some movement in this area," as the sergeant pointed to the locations on the map.

"Where is the closest team to their location?"

"None close enough. We just put them in a couple of days ago, and they were working up the AO toward the other teams. It would take eight to ten hours to move a team close to them, and who knows what they might run into on the way."

"That's not what I asked," barked the colonel.

"Yes, Sir," said the sergeant, pointing. "The closest team is Vapor Alpha, over here."

"Then we'll just have to count on air power," said the Colonel. "Keep me posted."

* * *

Back on the ground, it was a different situation. Angel team was set up on a small area of higher ground. They'd set up a perimeter of defense to keep any enemy at bay that might show up because of the fireworks. They had a good field of fire and a very defensible position, and there were no enemy combatants in sight. There was no gunfire, and they were only a short distance from an acceptable LZ location. The plan was in place.

"Aloft," called the RTO. "We need you to bring fire to our northwest. Can you pick up my shiny again?"

Terry looked down and searched through the general area where he knew the team should be. Just a little to the north of where he expected them, he saw the flash of sunlight from the mirror that the RTO was pointing at him. "Bravo, I have you," Terry called back. "I have a Spooky just coming in range. Would you like me to plow the field?"

"Go for it, Aloft. You know where we are. Please, just make sure they don't get too close to us."

"Roger that." Terry flipped his radio switches to the UHF and called the Spooky and told him to go up on a discreet frequency, switched over, then started giving direction.

"Four-Four," called Terry, "I have you in sight. I'm at your one o'clock position at 3,000 feet."

"Roger," came the reply. "Have you in sight."

"Okay, watch me," said Terry. "I'm going to show you where the team is. I'll fly over them at about 500 feet and call you when I'm right over head. Mark the spot well because that's what we'll use for a reference for weapons fire."

"Roger, copy that."

Terry rolled the Bird Dog upside-down and did a split-S dive toward the deck. The airspeed was approaching red-line as he started to pull out, then leveled out at about 700 feet MSL (Mean Sea Level)—which was about 300 feet above the deck. When he got near the team, he keyed his mike and called out "Five, four, three, two, one. Over the team. Do you copy, Four-Four?"

"Followed you the whole way, Aloft. If I pulled that maneuver, both my wings would come off. But we have your team marked."

"Okay, Four-Four—three-two-zero degrees and sixty meters. Rip 'em up." Terry was climbing hard and fast, turning back to watch the action. He saw the big old DC-3 heading toward the target. It flew over the team and started to make a circling bank to the right. Then, almost without warning, a stream of red light appeared, traveling from what would have been two passenger windows on the right side of the aircraft to the point on the ground that had been indicated by the team. Terry watched as the jungle seemed to be torn up, green leaves and branches flying around. A few seconds later and he could hear the distant hum of the gunfire as the twin Vulcan cannons ripped up the ground below. It was hard to believe that each of those guns was firing at 2600 rounds per minute, and every fifth round was a tracer. The tracers were the visible river of red. That was a lot of lead. Anything in that area, be it tree, jungle vine, or animal, would be completely destroyed in short order. It was almost like plowing a field.

The Cobra team was just arriving as the Spooky finished a second pass, and put some fire on the second location identified by the Angel Bravo team. They came up on frequency and called Terry as he continued to circle his Bird Dog, carefully watching where the guns were firing.

"Aloft, this is Snake One-Two. We have the Spooky working the area in sight. What do you need us to do?"

"Hang back for a couple of minutes while I check it out," said Terry as he answered over his second FM radio. He switched to his number one FM radio and called his Lerp team. "Bravo, what's going on down there?"

After an extended pause, the radio came alive. "Aloft, hold fire. The Spooky has shut 'em down for now, but we have to wait and see if there are any more out there. We have a couple of wounded though. I think you need to get some Slicks on the way. My God, that Spooky is amazing. Glad he's on our side."

* * *

Down below, Gabe was feeling bad. He hated lying about what was really going on, but he'd made up his mind. They had to create a couple of battle "injuries" to make it look real and get the medevac or Slicks on the way. Bart Blanks—BB for short—the pfc suffering with VD, was given a simulated shrapnel wound in the arm. "Now," Gabe had told him with a hint of humor in his voice, "you're gonna have a purple heart to go along with your purple balls." He shouted out to the rest of the team, "That deserves a round of applause," and the whole team clapped. Doc had volunteered to get the second wound. He already had two purple hearts, and with only two months left in country, this would get him a third, and a ticket out a little early. Gabe hated to lose him, but it was for a good cause—and he'd be off ground duty in another month anyway. *More army bullshit*, he thought as he bandaged BB. With all the morphine for his clap, BB hardly felt a thing when Gabe put the gash in his arm with his knife.

Terry had dutifully informed Oxide Vapor Control that they needed to pull the team out, and had gotten a promise that the Slicks would be dispatched in a couple of hours. It was the soonest they would be available. In the meantime, Terry was holding the Cobras just off to the east, on the other side of the op area from the Spooky.

"Aloft, Aloft, do you read?"

"Roger, this is Aloft."

"That area up to the northeast a few hundred yards looks good for an LZ for the extraction. Do you concur?"

"Give me a minute," Terry responded.

From his overhead position, Terry looked down at the team's location and at the clearing that the team was indicating. He flew a circle around the area and looked at the details. There was a tree-line on both sides that could cover the team as they came in position for the extraction. The problem was that the area was not cleared. Enemy could be there as well, and could ambush the team as they went into the open to board the helicopters.

"Angel, this is Aloft. Which way are you going to come into the LZ?"

"Aloft, this is Angel. Gabe says switch to maps."

Smart, thought Terry. *If the enemy's listening, they might figure it out and be waiting in ambush.* "Roger that," he radioed back.

"Aloft, this is Angel. We'll be Black Label plus five to plus six right eight to plus seven, then right eight and wait there. It'll take us about an hour and a half to get there, copy?"

Tim Ewell

Terry read back the planned route, then called it in to Oxide Vapor Control. They acknowledged and confirmed the ETA for the Slicks.

Now it was time for the mother hen to clear the road for his baby chick. His team did not need any surprises at this point. "Snake One-Three, this is Aloft."

"This is Snake One-Three, go ahead."

"I need you to clear an area for me. We just need to make sure we can move the team without resistance."

"Roger, where do you want us?"

"I'm going to give you some map points, and I want you to go see if you can find any activity. My team is going to be moving in for a lift-out, and we want the LZ clear before they get there."

"Copy that, Aloft. Go ahead with the map reading."

Terry gave him the instructions, then gave him a few minutes to get his bearings. Snake One-Three looked over the area he was given and called his teammate. "Snake One-Two, this is One-Three. I'll go low, you take high behind me. Let's see what we can wake up."

"Aloft, we're going to make a gun run. Keep an eye on us and let us know if you see anything."

"Roger that," Terry replied. He watched as Snake One-Three stopped his gunship in mid-air and almost came to a hover over the team. He was at about 2,000 feet. His teammate pulled up about a hundred yards behind him and slowed down as well. Then One-Three pointed his nose toward the ground and started a dive. At about a thousand feet above the jungle floor, he pulled the trigger on his mini-gun and ran a hundred-yard strafing pattern along what was to become the route that the LRRP team would need to take to get to the LZ. Snake One-Two followed the action from about 2,000 feet. There was no return fire. One-Two pulled a tight bank to the right, looking for activity below. Nothing.

"Aloft, this is One-Three. Looks like the path is clear. What next?"

"One-Three, this is Aloft. How long can you stay on station."

"About an hour and a half," he replied."

"Okay, One-Three. I still have the Spooky for cover. I'm expecting extraction at about . . . 1430. Can you be back about a half hour before that for cover?"

"Roger that, Aloft. Can't promise, but pretty sure that will work. We'll clear it with Oxide Vapor and see you then."

"Angel, this is Aloft. Say situation."

All was quiet on the ground when the RTO picked up his mike. He whispered out of habit. "Aloft. This is Angel. Two wounded, and we are starting our reposition to the LZ."

"Roger that," said Terry. "I have a Spooky on station while you're moving. Keep me posted. Any new enemy activity?"

"Negative, Aloft. I think you put 'em out of commission. At least for now."

The team had no idea, nor did anyone else, that two companies of NVA regulars had made their way into the area between the northern Lerp teams and the Angel Bravo team that was moving up from the south. The NVA were carrying mortars and RPGs for a combined and coordinated attack on the Bien Hoa Air Force Base later in the week. The team was approaching the LZ from the east. Unaware of the Angel team, the NVA had taken up a position to the west of the LZ under an area of fairly dense jungle. They'd heard the Spooky as it had been working an area about two klicks south and had taken cover, thinking they'd been spotted. But when the gunfire did not move toward them, they figured they would just lay low and be okay until night fall. At 1415 they watched as two Cobra gunships and a LOCH—a Hughes OH-6 observation helicopter, begin to circle overhead of the LZ.

Oxide Vapor Six, the colonel, was in the LOCH. He'd decided to come out of the TOC and check this out for himself. Lerp team

Angel Bravo had made its way to the east of the clearing that was to be used as the LZ.

The three Slicks were just pulling collective and settling to hover into the LZ when gunfire erupted. The NVA had a pretty good hint that they were going to see some activity in the clearing in front of them, and they had stealthily taken up positions just inside the tree line to wait. This was what any military man would call a target of opportunity. Yes, they had another mission, but the chance to take out men and machinery at the same time, and do it where they could watch it happen, was something they couldn't pass up.

Team Angel Bravo had just come into the clearing and were headed toward the Slicks. They were helping the wounded as they came, heard the gunfire, and all dropped to the ground.

Terry watched from above. He saw the smoke trail of an RPG come out of the jungle and barely miss the lead helicopter. His reaction was immediate. "This is Aloft," he yelled into his radio. "Enemy fire from the west. Get the Slicks airborne. Angel, take cover. Spooky is on his way."

He switched to his UHF. "Spooky, this is Aloft, just to the west of the LZ in the tree line, can you give me a little hell?" The old DC-3 that had been orbiting off a few miles away answered that they were on the way.

Terry switched back to the FM radio. "One-Three, this is Aloft. I need a run on that tree line before the spooky gets here."

"Roger that, Aloft, One-Three and One-Two going in."

The two Cobra gunships were overhead when the arms fire had erupted below. They were just waiting for coordination. They dove at the tree line side by side, two rivers of red spewing from the mini-guns that were located on the pylons on either side of the aircraft.

The Hueys were now moving at high hover, just going through translational lift as they fought to get airborne and out of the LZ. Another RPG came screaming out of the darkness of the jungle tree line. This time the Slicks weren't so lucky. The round caught the tail boom of the trailing helicopter, and without a tail rotor—and hence torque control—it slowly began to spin. It only had about thirty feet to fall, and the pilot did all he could to cushion the landing, but it hit pretty hard and rolled on its side, bringing its big rotor blades to a hard stop. Pieces of the blades flew across the LZ, barely missing the Lerp team.

Team members were now crawling back toward the tree line they'd come from—a more defensive location. *Damn*, Gabe was thinking. *The best laid plans—at least now it's all for real.*

Spooky came in and began to work over the suspected enemy position. The Cobras fired a few high-explosive rockets and some 30-mm into the area. It took about twenty minutes for things to get quiet again. The Slicks had taken up positions about three miles away from the LZ. and were waiting for further orders. The decision was made to bring the remaining two back in, to pick up the team and any helicopter survivors. In the meantime, a medevac helicopter had come in as well. Between the three of them, and with the help of the Lerp team, they were able to pull the four crew members out of the downed chopper. The right side gunner had been crushed when the helicopter rolled over and was barely alive. They all had broken bones, cuts, and bruises. They took them out on stretchers and put them on the medevac chopper. The pilot of the downed Slick kept insisting that someone go back and hit the "Zero Out" switch on his bird and kept saying something about the ZYR/ZYS box. The copilot of the rescue bird heard him and quickly got out of his seat and ran over to the upside-down helicopter and flipped the zeroize switch. The radio encoder with its secrets was now useless to the enemy. The rest of the men piled into the two remaining Slicks, and as the copilot jumped back in his seat, put on his helmet, and fastened his seatbelt as the pilot beeped up his engine to 6600 rpm, pulled pitch, and they were on their way home.

Oxide Vapor Six had watched the whole thing without saying a word. Everyone had done their job pretty well. Spooky had been released and was on his way back to Ben Hoa for fuel and ammo, and probably a crew change.

Terry recognized the commanding voice when it came on the radio. "Aloft, this is Oxide Vapor Six."

"Yes, Sir," Terry responded.

"That was pretty good initiative finding the Spooky and all. You kept your wits about you. Are you the same pilot I was talking to last night about the kid with the clap?"

"Yes, Sir, that would be me." Terry was careful speaking to this arrogant ass.

"You get two things out of this, 'cause it was a job well done. One, I forget about last night; and two, you get a medal."

"No need, Sir," said Terry, "but thanks anyway."

"Not a career officer, are you, Son. Never mind. Aloft, as long as you're still here, can you give us a little cover? We're going to take a look at the area we just hit. Me and the snakes are going to play a little hunter-killer. Keep an eye on us. I'm confident you can do that."

"Roger Sir, as you wish."

God, how stupid, thought Terry. *The battalion commander is a fucking cowboy.* Terry knew what hunter-killer meant—that the OH-6 helicopter, which looked like an overgrown bumble bee would be the hunter and go down to the jungle floor for a look-see. Then if it found any action or took fire, the Cobras, with all their firepower, would come in from above and clean house.

By now Spooky had already been released and was headed back to Bien Hoa. Terry heard Six call Snake One-Three and set up an attack plan, and he watched as the LOCH headed for the LZ. He watched as the LOCH hovered around the clearing, looking for dead enemy. The Cobras circled like vultures overhead.

What he did not know is that the commander of the NVA force that they'd just encountered had only committed a six-man team to the LZ and had pulled the rest of his 300 soldiers back out of the area about a click west, saving them for the upcoming attack on Bien Hoa.

Terry watched in almost disbelief as the LOCH started to dip under the triple canopy jungle. "We're following a trail," came the radio call, and then they disappeared.

"Snake, this is Aloft. Do you have them in sight?"

"We watched 'em go in. Can't see 'em."

Just then they heard the radio come alive as a panicked Oxide Vapor Six keyed his mike and yelled, "We're taking fire!"

So what did you expect? thought Terry. The sound of automatic gunfire could be heard in the background. And then the most amazing thing happened. Up through the trees—seriously, straight up through the triple canopy—came the LOCH helicopter, cutting limbs from trees and leaves and vines like an egg beater as it made a panicked climb out of the jungle.

Once they were clear of the tallest trees and beginning to move across the top of the canopy, the Cobras, without waiting for further orders, started their attack. As they were working the area over, Six came on the line. "Aloft, we have some damage and have to go back. We're going to have Snake escort us back just in case. I'm ordering an Arc Light for that area. In the meantime, see what you can do to keep 'em busy down there. For your info, that is a large force. I'd say a hundred or more. I'll be back."

"Yes, Sir," Terry responded. "By the way, I've never seen anything like that before. You should give your pilot the medal."

From the Loch, Six said, "Right, Aloft, I agree." He then looked down at the Plexiglas bubble below the pilot's feet and saw a small puddle of red. Then he saw the rip in the thigh of his uniform. "You all right?" he asked the pilot.

"No, Sir," he said. " Do you think you could put a bandage or something on that and stop the bleeding?" His voice was calm, but Six could hear the grimace as the pilot spoke through his gritted teeth. The CO tore off his shirt, then pulled off his OD-green tee-shirt and ripped it from top to bottom. He made another tear and then another creating green strips. He wrapped them along with the rest of his shirt onto the pilot's leg, made a knot, and cinched it.

"How long till base?" he asked the pilot.

"Don't think I can make base, Sir. Can you fly this thing?"

"No, Soldier, I can't. Just do the best you can. You'll make it." Then he radioed a Cobra. "Snake, this is Six. My pilot took a round in the leg and is losing blood. Got any suggestions?"

Terry listened as the drama unfolded. He was helpless. The Cobras pulled up alongside the little LOCH like two huge wasps alongside a honey bee. While they flew, the pilot showed the commander the basics of the controls. Of all the helicopters made, with its power–to–weight ratio, its automatic speed governor, and four rotor blades, it was one of the easiest to fly.

"If your pilot loses consciousness, we'll try to talk you to base. It's all we can do," said One-Three.

"Aloft Three-Four, this is Aloft Three-Nine." Terry had almost lost track of time. He had another Spooky on the way, a potential Arc Light coming, more gunships being dispatched, and he had forgotten that he was nearly out of fuel and had to return to base. Aloft Three-Nine was his relief.

It took Terry almost ten minutes to brief Three-Nine about what was going on, where the teams were, what was expected, and what grid coordinates to fire on. There was even a 155 mm howitzer battery that was being redirected at the location. He gave him the gun line coordinates for that. He was almost back to Phu Loi before he finished giving Three-Nine instructions.

He heard later that the colonel's LOCH had landed safely. The pilot managed to stay alert despite the loss of blood, and the medics were on the ramp waiting for him. He passed out as they were helping him out of his seat. They got him to the base hospital quickly, where they patched him up. It sounded like he was going to be all right.

True to his word, Six put his LOCH pilot in for a Distinguished Flying Cross and a Purple Heart, both of which were awarded just before he was sent home. It would take him over a year to recuperate.

Chapter 12

They'd barely driven through the entrance to the orphanage, just passed the old white plastered walls, when children seemed to appear out of nowhere. Ranging in ages from about three to eleven or twelve, and all ages, sizes, and colors in between, they converged on the Jeep. Ski stopped in the center of the large, dusty square courtyard, and before he could raise his leg up to climb out, one little boy was pulling at the sleeve of his flight suit.

"*Dai wi . . . Dai wi*"—Vietnamese for "captain," he shouted it over the noise of the other children. They all knew who he was and that when he came to visit, special things happened—things like candy and Kool-Aid.

"Hang on, Terry," he said as he carefully worked himself out of the Jeep to a standing position. By now he was surrounded by twenty-five or thirty smiling kids, all speaking in excited voices, in a language Terry couldn't understand, and all crowding in as close as they could. Ski didn't speak Vietnamese either, but he did have a language they seemed to understand. It was in his eyes and his caring voice.

Just a short distance away, in the archway to the main door of the orphanage, a figure dressed in black stood watching. Standing just back in the shadow of the archway, it was hard to make out who or what was there. It caught Terry's eye, and he cautiously reached for his Colt .45, which was always at the ready in his shoulder holster. Ski saw the motion, glanced up, and saw the reason for his concern. He shook his head as if to say "put it back," and made a motion to the figure in the doorway. As she came out toward the Jeep, it was easy to see the reason for the mistake and why Ski was so unconcerned. The nun was dressed in a traditional black–and–white habit and was certainly adult in size. She came over, and the children parted to let her approach.

"Well, Captain, I see you made it through once again." She smiled as she spoke, and there was obvious anticipation in her voice.

"Not that far to go," said Ski, "and it's my day off." He was lying. He was scheduled to fly that night, and should have been getting some much needed sleep, but something had made him want to be here instead. Now with his surprise package, it was even more important.

"How are the kids doing?" he asked.

"As you can see, just fine," she replied. "Happy and healthy, a lot thanks to you. And who have you brought with you today?"

"Oh, sorry. Sister Evon, this is Captain—I mean, this is Terry. He's another one of the pilots up at the Eighty-ninth. He's come to see your place and meet some of the kids."

Terry nodded at the sister, and she smiled and nodded back.

"By the way, I have a special package for you today," said Ski.

"What did the army donate to our worthwhile cause this time?"

The sisters were amazing. They'd founded this orphanage when the French were in control, and had seen the need to keep it up when the French pulled out and the Americans took over. So they stayed, despite a lot of hardship. They were really caught between two worlds because of these special kids. They weren't just abandoned or orphaned. A lot of these kids were part "round eyes"—not fully Vietnamese, but children of the occupation, fathered by men who'd come and gone. They were hated by full-blooded Vietnamese and left behind by the fathers, who often didn't even know of their existence. The mothers of these children, and the helpless children themselves, were abused, sometimes murdered, by the VC and NVA. They were treated as enemies—or even worse, as traitors. So to protect the children—and themselves—the mothers brought them to the orphanage.

The actual buildings had been built by the French as the main home for a rubber plantation. It was well built compared to most of the regular buildings and homes in this part of the country. It was well suited for its present purpose. As the war progressed, the rubber trees were destroyed by the same defoliants being used to eliminate the jungle. The French had given the entire plantation to the sisters, and at the orphanage, they were left alone. It was neutral, a kind of no-man's land or DMZ. The sisters prayed daily that it would stay that way.

Taking advantage of this apparent peace, the sisters put together a special program to give the children a starting point for the tough world they would someday have to face—that is, if they could just reach maturity. They had classes in language and history and math, classes that most of the children in the villages would never get. The sisters believe that if they had skills, they could find a place in society—even though they didn't look the same as their peers.

Sister Ellen came through the shadowy archway at the front of the orphanage into the bright courtyard, carrying an infant girl on her hip.

Ski worked his way to the back of the Jeep and loosened the ropes on three wooden crates. "Here, help me with these," he said with a grunt as he strained to lift the first one out.

The sisters corralled the kids and made them sit down on the steps leading to the archway entrance while Ski and Terry unloaded the crates from the back of the Jeep. They weren't real heavy, but they were bulky and it was easier with the two of them. They carried them over to the entrance to the kitchen, with Sister Evon guiding the way. A couple of the older children were instructed to take them from there to the cook inside.

"Of course you know that these two crates are C-Rations," Ski said to Sister Evon as they walked back to the Jeep, where Sister Louise joined them to help. "The last one is special You asked for toys for the kids. Well, we got a few, and some English readers. That was a lot harder, but there's a few here. And Pop sent some linens and blankets. He says he'll get some more for you as soon as he can."

What he didn't mention was how he'd had everyone back in the company writing home to ask for toys. For the last two weeks, almost every package of goodies from home had at least one toy inside. Sister Ellen, and Sister Louise fairly beamed with joy.

Ski was in his element. The kids loved him and he loved the kids—every one of them. You could see it on their faces. The things he and Pop scrounged for the orphanage helped get them by.

The children went back to playing games and doing the things that kids enjoy, while the adults exchanged the latest war gossip. There wasn't much new to tell really. The basics hadn't changed much in the last twenty years.

"What did you do with the new arrival we brought you a couple of weeks ago?" Ski asked.

"You mean that one who . . . arrived by helicopter? That was kind of unusual for us."

Sister Ellen motioned to Sister Louise, who quietly got up and went into the main house. She was gone only a minute, then reappeared carrying Nguyen. He still had a small bandage on the back of his head.

"Funny thing about this boy," said Sister Ellen. "He talks a lot."

"Yes, so I've heard. Too bad I don't speak Vietnamese," said Ski.

"Obviously you haven't been told," she said slyly. "It would be better if you spoke French. He is practically fluent."

A look of amazement came over Ski's face. "What are you talking about?"

"Well, he speaks Vietnamese too, but when he got here and heard us talking to each other in French, his eyes lit up, and we could not stop him from telling his story."

Terry looked at Ski.

Ski asked if he could hold the boy, and Sister Ellen obliged by picking him up and putting him in his lap. To Ski, it was as if the war had taken a brief recess. Something he'd always wanted, even longed for, was his for a moment. If only . . . but he knew it was a long shot.

The little blue-eyed boy seemed to recognize Ski, and he became more at ease. Being with people who understood his language was probably more comfortable for him.

"Terry," he said slowly, "what do you think of the name 'Bobby'? He looks more like my Bobby to me, don't you agree?"

"Sure, Ski," Terry agreed, confused.

"Wouldn't it be great if we could get him out of this place?"

"The orphanage is better than a village or the jungle right now, Ski, don't you think?"

"That's not what I was thinking about," Ski said as the kids continued to come over to smile and touch him, their way of thanking him. "Oh well . . . just a dream."

When things quieted down, Terry asked, "What did you mean when you said your 'Bobby'?"

"Just a figure of speech, Terry. I want to take him home with me," he said, matter-of-factly.

"Okay, Armanski—you're certifiable now! I'll call the flight surgeon when we get back to Phu Loi and he'll send you home, no problem."

"No, listen to me. Look at this kid. He's beautiful. I wrote home to Barbara and told her about him. I even told her I'd send her a picture. She's wild about the idea. Since we can't have kids of our own, we're going to adopt Bobby."

The look in his eyes told Terry that his friend Ski was very serious, and this was not something to joke about. He said, "In case you haven't noticed, Ski, this is a war zone. What are you gonna do—take him home in your duffel bag?"

"I have my ways," answered Ski. "Pop's due to go home in four months, and we have a plan."

This took Terry by surprise, but it explained a lot about Ski. It was almost a foregone conclusion. "Okay," he said, disbelief in his voice. "Step one. Get the Sisters to agree."

"Already done," Ski said. "They figure his chances here are poor, regardless of the war. Besides, they need the space. They'll help any way they can to give him a better chance at a real life."

"Okay now, you gotta get him on a plane. It's the only way out of here. How ya gonna do that?"

"That's where Pop comes in. He's working on the ultimate scrounge deal. We'll know in a few weeks."

"Pop is working on a deal that I don't know about? That's kind of hard to believe," said Terry.

"Pop is pretty good with secrets if he needs to be," said Ski.

"Ok, well yeah, that's true," answered Terry. Then he said. "What about immigration? They're not going to let this kid into the states. Say you get him there. They'll just send him back."

The boy sat on Ski's knee and listened to the whole conversation intently. He was only six, but although the sisters had started teaching him English, he didn't know what the conversation was all about. He just knew he liked Ski.

They left the orphanage about an hour later. The ride home was pretty quiet. Terry asked a few questions, and Ski gave him a few short answers. All in all, Terry could tell it was something that Ski had thought about and worked on a lot. Pop kept coming up in the conversation. He was obviously the key to making this whole thing happen. But how? Terry was convinced that Ski was pretty sure he'd come up with a way to pull it off. He liked a challenge, but he could also imagine the court martial when they got caught.

Did I say something to suggest I was going to help with this? Terry wondered. *Well* . . .

Terry figured he saw the vision. It would be neat to try. And what could they do to them if they failed and got busted—send them to Vietnam? Yeah, probably—and as grunts. Oh well, *que sera, sera.*

Chapter 13

"One small step for a man, one giant leap for mankind." Neil Armstrong had just set foot on the moon. The war in Vietnam was escalating. Secret missions were being flown into Cambodia and Laos, in preparation for what was to be a major assault to cut the enemy supply lines. No one thought much about how the US could manage to go to the moon and wage war at the same time. In retrospect, it had to be a lot like fighting a two-front war. The US had spent a massive amount of money on a successful mission to go to the moon—and was spending an ever-increasing amount on a war that seemed to be going nowhere.

For many of the men involved in the war, life had settled into a kind of routine. Base camps like Phu Loi were fairly stable places. There were barber shops, a PX, mess halls and routine inspections. There were Officers' and Enlisted Men's Clubs equipped with dance floors and TV sets. You knew you were not at home, but those who were stationed at these places found it wasn't all that hard to take. Rarely did the enemy try to attack these bases. Every few nights there would be an obligatory rocket or mortar attack, but damage was usually minor. One night a mortar round blew up the company water tower. They had it rebuilt in two hours the next day. The exploding shell had sent a piece of hot shrapnel into one of the hooches, where a group of Bird Dog mechanics was sleeping. It went into the pillow just under one mans head. He woke up with his face burning hot and not knowing why until they found the piece of charred metal in the pillow. Another lucky miss.

Out in the field, on patrol, in the fire bases, life was much different. Those living there were under constant assault. The enemy didn't like having US troops in their territory, and their ongoing attacks were a reminder of their presence—a reminder of their determination to rid their land of the so-called invaders.

The pilots who flew from the secure base camps out into the remote reaches of South Vietnam saw both worlds—safe on their base when not on duty, and in the thick of the action when flying their missions. They lived with the units they flew support for, sometimes days at a time, sometimes weeks or months at a time. A base camp was like the US, in a primitive sort of way. But when out in the area of operations, it was war. It was the first all-out guerilla war in US history, and there were a lot of hard lessons to be learned. And just like in the wars before them, the lessons usually came at the cost of many dedicated lives.

* * *

Major Pratt was sitting at his desk doing the same things he would be doing if he were at a stateside job. He reviewed personnel records, and checked the first sergeant's recommendations for incoming newcomer assignments. He kept track of the unit safety statistics and reviewed the pilots' missions. Not a lot to do, really. Just keep everyone happy and doing their job. Solve the little problems before they became big problems. And as the war dragged on, certain things were evident. There was a growing uneasiness among his pilots. He couldn't really put a finger on it, but it was there.

That evening, as the routine workday drew to a close, he walked down the concrete path from his office to the Officers' Quarters, which was directly adjacent to the Officers' Club. Between the buildings was the underground sleeping bunker.

He recalled that not long ago they were all sleeping down there rather than in the nice above-ground, concrete-block hooches. With the semi-stability they now enjoyed, the move to above-ground quarters had become feasible.

He walked by Nude Nelson's room just as Nude was finishing a counseling session with a young private, one of the mechanics who worked on the Bird Dogs. As usual, he was sitting on the edge of his bunk, buck naked and telling this poor kid, who was practically in tears, how to deal with an unfaithful wife back home.

Damn, he thought, *what the hell is he doing? This isn't a nudist colony and the kid deserves some dignity. Maybe he should say something to Nelson's section leader.* But instead, he just walked on.

Adjacent to the bunker was a rectangular space of land covered with grass and surrounded by a concrete walkway. It was a great spot for barbecues, or just sitting out and sipping a cool one on a hot afternoon.

Pratt went to his room and took off his fatigue shirt, then removed his hat and tossed them both on the bunk. He stepped back out into the muggy Vietnam evening and started across the grassy spot toward the Officers' Club. His white tee-shirt was in stark contrast to his olive green fatigue pants and shiny black combat boots. Terry was just returning from the mess hall, and they met as they passed the old bunker.

"Evening, Sir," said Terry as he raised his hand in a smart salute.

"Evening, Capt. Downey. Where ya headed?"

"Just to my hooch to write a letter or read a magazine or something. Just to get into a cooler place for a while. Nothing important, sir."

"Sit down a minute, Terry," Pratt said in a friendly tone. "I want to talk a bit, okay?"

"Yes Sir. What about?"

They sat down on the top of the bunker facing the Officers' Club. From inside you could hear the sounds of several of the pilots who'd been drinking for a while and were starting to get happy. After all, what else was there to do when the missions of the day were complete?

"Terry, did you ever see a movie called *Away All Boats*?" Major Pratt decided not to tell Terry what the movie was about.

Terry thought for a moment, then said, "Don't remember that one."

Pratt was talking about a WWII film about the captain of a boat carrying landing craft—about kamikaze attacks on a navy ship and how it survived. But it was really a lesson in leadership. The captain had officers and men who were not getting along with each other. He gave them a reason to put their hatred on him—and build camaraderie between each other. He told them they had to build him a sailboat. At the time they were overwhelmed with their day-to-day work, and adding this superfluous task to their already long days seemed like an unnecessary burden.

Now Major Pratt could see some of the same attitudes developing with his flying officers, and he thought he might be able to come up with a way to do something to get them working together, have a common enemy, and have something that, when completed, would make them feel proud. And it would be something that they could enjoy.

"It doesn't really matter," said Major Pratt. "The point is, you were making some remarks about maybe building a swimming pool over there"—he pointed, in front of the Officers' Quarters—"right there in front of the old bunker in the grassy spot."

"Yes, Sir," answered Terry. "It would be the perfect place."

"Do you still think it can be done?"

"Just give me the go-ahead, Sir, and I'll show you what can be done. We can trade the base engineers for construction equipment. Pop has a line on some filtration equipment. I know where there's some surplus cement. Yes, Sir—we can do it if you give it the okay."

"What are you going to trade to the engineers?" Pratt paused. "Never mind. I'm better off not knowing. You realize you're probably going to meet some opposition from the other officers. That bother you?"

"It's okay, Sir. When the water is in the pool, they'll appreciate it."

"All right. Do it. Now, how long do you think it will take?"

"I'm not sure, Sir, but give me a couple of days and I'll give you a good estimate. It's probably a two-month job, but I'll let you know."

"Good," Major Pratt said softly before turning to walk toward the club. Then he looked back at Terry. "Take your time and make it a good pool."

"Yes, Sir."

* * *

The next day, Terry took a walk around to the engineers' area. He'd been there many times before. There was a particular lieutenant who'd been helpful in the past and was not afraid to do a few favors if he could get a favor or two in return.

"So my CO says to me, can you build a pool?" said Terry. "We have a great place for it. We just need to dig the hole."

"And you need me for what?" asked the engineer.

"Ah, come on, I just need to use some of your heavy equipment, stuff you're not using anyway, and I just need it for a couple of days."

"Like what?"

"How about a front-loader?"

"Possible, but you'll have to use my operator."

"Fair enough," said Terry. "We may also need to borrow a transit and a few other hand tools, if that works."

"I think that can be arranged easy enough."

"Now, what can I do for you?" asked Terry.

The lieutenant thought for a minute. "Any suggestions?" he said.

"How about a couple of R&R flights to Vung Tau?"

"Not bad . . . okay. Think you can set that up in the next couple of weeks?"

"I think that can be arranged easy enough," he said, echoing the lieutenant. "Just give me times and dates. I'll even make it better. I'll take up to four troops at a time, and you can sell off the extra seats for bargaining chips to whoever you want." Terry was thinking about the Beaver and how he could take it out on a "training flight" about any time he wanted. Flying to Vung Tau was about an hour and a half. No big deal.

"Not bad. I like working with you," said the lieutenant.

"I aim to please," said Terry. "I just need you to help me out as I work through this project. What do you say?"

* * *

"Ski, we have a bonus here. Help me with the guys so they help with the pool," begged Terry.

"Why?" asked Ski.

"Look at all the things we can do. We can scrounge, we can trade, and if we're questioned, which we won't be, but if we are, we can just say it's for the pool."

Steve arched his eyebrows. "Okay, that's a good idea. But you're still going to catch hell."

"Does it matter for the big picture?" Terry said.

"So when do we start?"

"As soon as the hole diggers get here."

A couple of days later, the front loader arrived at the entrance to the compound, and the driver followed Terry back to the Officers' Quarters. There, they used the hydraulic bucket and picked up the brick barbecue that had been built in the grassy area next to the club. They carefully moved it onto the top of the underground bunker, which was where the new patio and diving board would be located.

Everyone was pretty skeptical. No one wanted to take any of their precious time off and spend it working on a pool. They just wanted to sit around the club, play poker, and drink. But the CO had made it clear. They would build the pool, and every officer would get involved.

The aviation ranks were different then. Although an officer might be a pilot, he was also part of a branch of service. In other words, there were Infantry Officers, Engineer Officers, Artillery Officers, Signal officers, Armor officers, and others. Each branch had its specialties. Since this was really an engineering project—at least in the beginning—much of the responsibility fell to Lt. Saunders, Engineer. He would help in the design and structure, to make sure it was built properly. It wasn't what he wanted to do, but once he got into it, he seemed to enjoy it. When they got down to the manual labor, everyone pitched in. It was good exercise, and although there were some complaints, it was something to do. And doing something worthwhile gave each person a certain sense of accomplishment. The drinking slowed down, but only a little. Some of them just switched from the hard stuff to cold beer.

Pop scrounged up some rebar for reinforcing the concrete. Terry traded out another trip to Vung Tau for cement. Before long, the project took on a life of its own. Other guys were coming up with ideas and finding things for the pool. Saunders became the leader and made them follow his plans precisely. He told Terry what he needed, and Terry did his best to scrounge things up. He got a lot of flack from some of the guys for even suggesting the project, but it was the CO who caught most of the grief. No one would complain to his face, but a lot of the officers grumbled behind his back.

At the same time, Ski was still working on the plan for getting "Bobby" out of the country. He still pulled his time on the pool and flew his missions. But the plan, and the little blue-eyed boy, were where his heart was.

Chapter 14

Pop had his eyes on an air force Beaver that was "off the books." It had been built from three other Beavers that had crashed. They'd pulled the main fuselage from one, the wings from another, and the tail section from a third. When the parts were assembled, it was as good as new. For the guys who'd put it together, it was a lot like the swimming pool project. It was something to do that was outside the military routine, and when they were done, it was something they could look at and be proud of. As far as the air force was concerned, it did not exist. When they left country, they gave the plane to their maintenance chief.

The Beaver was the big secret and key to Pop's plan. Major Snyder, the officer who had it, was in charge of field maintenance at Bien Hoa. He wasn't even a rated pilot, but he'd bootlegged enough instruction time to be able to fly it pretty well, which he did about once a week. He and a few other fellow air force officers would fly down to Saigon to the Officers' Club for Sunday morning champagne brunch. That's where Pop had met him.

Over the months since their meeting, they'd made a lot of deals. Snyder's outfit took care of a lot of different kinds of airplanes: the DC-3, called "Puff the Magic Dragon" or "Spooky," jet fighters—and even the Cessna O-2, a highly modified Cessna Skymaster. The O-2, with its engines in front and back, and its split boom tail, was called the poor man's P-38. It was the air force's choice for a forward observer airplane. They still had a few Bird Dogs and some Beavers though. That's where the two units had common ground.

Whenever Terry went to Bien Hoa, he always stopped by Major Snyder's office. Snyder was a large, easy-going guy who seemed to have plenty of time for him or Pop. Over at the Eighty-ninth, they had a real problem with fouling spark plugs. The Lerp mission was particularly hard on them because the pilots flew at economy power, and it just seemed to load up the spark plugs with carbon. Then they'd misfire and make the engine run rough. The air force used a different kind of plug, one the maintenance guys called a "massive," which seemed to work better for the slow flight missions. The army's was called a "fine wire." Major Snyder tried his best to order extra plugs, and usually had a box or two on hand for the army pilots when they came by. There was no big inter-service rivalry over there—at least not among the guys at Terry's level. Maybe the generals had their power struggles, but the ordinary troops just had their job to do, and they did it the best they could. Because the air force was trying to phase out the O-1 Bird Dog, they had some supply shortages in areas where the army supply had some surplus. Sometimes they needed a cylinder or plug wires or a magneto. Pop and Terry helped them out.

Terry didn't know why Pop was so hot on that Beaver, except that it was something he could fly while the OV-1 just sat on the ramp. Pop eventually worked the trade. It was a four-way swap involving the Mohawk unit at Vung Tao, an R&R slot in Hawaii, some parachutes, and a Walther PPK pistol. There was also a side deal promising to deliver something somewhere, but Pop was mum on that.

They were lucky that the CO turned a blind eye to all this. But it seemed that Pop had some bargaining material there, too—and the CO, only a major, didn't dare mess with the arrangement.

Major Pratt rarely came down to the flight line, so when the new Beaver showed up, he didn't even notice. Pop had made arrangements with the 101st Maintenance Group to repaint it from air force camouflage blue to army olive drab. He put the

Recon Airplane Company: III Corps, Vietnam

same tail numbers on it as on the company Beaver, and kept them parked far enough apart so that no one paid much attention.

Whenever there was an inspection, he would taxi it down to one of the other company areas, or take it over to battalion HQ at Long Than and park it there. No one ever caught on. The maintenance crew kept it in top-notch shape. It was the pride of the unit. Pop scrounged everything he could for it and quietly had it installed. It had two ADF radios, an HF radio, two UHF radios, and two FM radios. Somewhere he found a VOR receiver, and he put that in too. The air force had put in upgraded flight instruments, and Pop filled in the copilot's panel with upgraded equipment as well.

It was fitted with long-range wing tip fuel tanks, but they were rarely used. It had a plush interior with padded seats instead of the old army bucket and sling seats. It was a real show piece.

It had a nearly new Pratt & Whitney R-985 engine when Pop had gotten it from the air force, and it ran as smooth as a Rolls. Pop and Terry used it for a lot of their scrounging missions. With the rear seats out, they could carry just about anything. The nice thing about a Beaver was that if you could get whatever it was you had to fit on board, you could probably get in the air with it. It was truly a STOL (Short Take-Off and Landing) aircraft. It was made by De Havilland of Canada, the same company that made the Otter and the Caribou, both also well-known STOL planes.

A couple of the company pilots knew that Pop had special plans for the Beaver, but he wouldn't tell anyone what they were. For now it was just his special toy. When he left country, he would have to trade it for something, hopefully get some cash. That was how things usually worked.

But things didn't always turn out as expected or planned—and the amazing Pop and his Beaver would probably surprise everyone.

Chapter 15

The missions changed from day to day and week to week. One week, Terry might have a three-day stint in Tay Ninh, and then be flying the "Moon River" mission in the Run Sat Special Zone. He liked the Moon River mission because he liked the observer who normally flew with him—Marine Lieutenant Don Moss. He'd been a gunnery sergeant when he'd first come to Vietnam six years ago, had been promoted to first sergeant, and had then received a direct commission to lieutenant. He was big, like a football linebacker. And he was a tough boss. But he treated the pilots who flew him around like they were royalty.

Terry flew into Tan Son Nhut at daybreak. He landed and taxied down Charlie taxiway to the main north-south taxiway that led to the south ramp, which was an air force FAC (Forward Air Controller) staging area. There was a small trailer there where pilots sat and drank coffee and played poker between flights. That's where he always met Lt. Moss. As a captain, Terry outranked Moss, but his time in service and time in the battle zone put them on a less than equal footing. Terry was a good pilot, better than most. It was to be expected—he'd been flying ever since he was sixteen years old, and he was a natural. He understood aerodynamics and mechanics, and he knew his Bird Dog inside and out. But when Moss wanted him to do something or fly a particular way, he did it. Moss had been there. He knew what it took to get the job done. They made a good team.

Before he arrived on the ramp, Terry would perform a little ritual. Company policy didn't allow Bird Dog pilots to carry ordnance, except for smoke marking rockets. Not many of them lived by that rule, except Mile High Milford, who wouldn't do anything to risk his neck or to save anyone else's. Terry pulled the plane up to the rocket loading ramp, shut down the engine, and climbed out. Several air force types were wandering around the area, but no one paid any attention to him. He was just another guy in uniform doing a job. He hooked up a ground wire to the launch tubes under the left wing, then checked the cockpit to make sure all the firing switches were off and the red safeties down. The master switch was off and the trigger safety pin was in place.

He walked back to the rear of the rocket tube and, standing to one side, pivoted the firing electrode away from the rear of one of the white phosphorous rockets they called Willie Petes in the tube. He pulled the detent mechanism and slid the four-foot, twenty-five-pound rocket out of the launch tube and laid it on the ground.

After both left-side rockets were safely on the ground, he went to the bunker about twenty feet away and retrieved two HE (High Explosive) warhead rockets and slid them into the tubes as replacements for the WPs. Then he took the Willy Petes and put them in the storage bunker.

He had just finished reloading and setting the firing mechanism when Moss arrived. He was in a marine Jeep driven by a lance corporal. He pulled up behind the plane and said, "Good mornin', Sir. Nice day for huntin' Charlie, don't ya think?" He got out of his Jeep and stretched.

"Right, Don," Terry answered. "I'm set if you are."

"Now let's not be in a big hurry. You had coffee yet?"

"No." Terry said. He liked the idea.

"Okay, let's get some first, and I'll go over the map with you."

They started toward the trailer, but Don turned to look at his driver. "Deaver?" he said in a commanding voice. "I want this Jeep washed before you pick me up at 1600. Got that?"

"But, Sir," whimpered the lance corporal, "you know we have a water shortage. They're rationing. I can't possibly get it washed today."

Don's features stiffened, and he bent over and looked Corporal Deaver in the eye. "I don't care if you have to piss on it—it'll be clean by 1600 hours."

Don turned back to Terry and they resumed walking toward the line shack trailer. The Jeep drove slowly away, its driver shaking his head and shrugging. "Kid needs a little discipline and direction. Best driver I ever had though." Then, without missing a beat, he said, "You gonna put some real stuff in the tubes today, Cap'n?"

* * *

At that time, Tan Son Nhut was the busiest airport in the world. It wasn't unusual to be number sixteen to land behind a flight of seven C-130s and a flight of eight C-7 caribous. It was almost as hard to get a takeoff slot—unless you had a trick, and Terry had one. There was a taxiway called "Charlie" that was at its farthest end, and out at the end was a ramp for parking airplanes called "Charlie Row." Terry taxied toward it, and as he got close, he'd switch to tower frequency and call "Aloft Three-Two, ready for takeoff, Charlie." And if there was a space, they'd clear him for takeoff, not realizing he was still quite a way from the runway. The taxiway entered the runway at about a thirty-degree angle, and it was about 600 feet from its entrance at Charlie Row to where the runway began. The minute he had clearance, he applied full power, accelerated down the taxiway, and would be off the ground before he got to the runway. Then he made a hard left bank, almost scraping the wing on the designated takeoff runway, and level off at full speed in the takeoff direction, five feet above the runway. The American controllers loved this maneuver and never gave it a second thought. The Vietnamese controllers, who moved much slower, got very frustrated, and Terry couldn't understand their angry broken English as they radioed him just before he cleared the end of the runway, climbed to a hundred feet or so, and headed for the Saigon River.

Moss always laughed at this maneuver and told him that he was the best pilot he knew at getting off the Saigon Airport without delay. It felt good to be appreciated.

* * *

Back in the operations bunker at Phu Loi, Puck was back on duty. The phone on his desk rang. He took his feet off the desk and casually reached over to answer it. "Operations, Spec Four Hull," he said firmly.

"Hull, this is the XO. Where do you have Downey flying today?"

Where do I have Downey flying today? Hull thought. *As if I give the orders. Listen boss, I just try to keep track of those crazy flyboys.* He looked up at his control board. "I show him on Moon River today, Sir."

"Can you raise him on the UHF?" said the XO.

"Let's see . . ." He looked at the status board. "I spoke to him about thirty minutes ago. He was landing at Saigon to pick up an observer. Probably be able to get him within the hour, Sir."

"Right. Give it a try and let me know when you have him. I want to talk to him."

"Yes, Sir."

When the XO hung up, Puck put his feet back on the desk and picked up his book of Shakespeare's major plays. "Alas, herewith I sit, in comfort. Yea, but upon what purpose doth this body repose in such a contort manner? But to read of knights and loves of old? Of tragedy that doth oft unfold when everywhere around my conscious core, tragedy is written by the very day and hour; and heart grows cold if oft the loss is felt of friend and comrade." He sat up, picked up his pencil, and wrote down the passage. He would memorize that for future use.

Then he replayed the conversation with the XO in his head. *I wonder what Terry's done to piss off the old man*, he thought. *He really sounded like it was urgent.*

* * *

As they flew over the southern edge of the city, they could see Marine Headquarters below them. It was just a little jut of land sticking out into the river with a couple of buildings and a PSP-covered helipad.

"Someday I'll land you on that pad in this plane, Moss" Terry said over the intercom.

"Anytime you want to try, Sir, I'll go with you. But remember—it's only 300 feet square."

"No sweat, but not today. I guess you have some work for us," Terry said.

"Roger that," said Moss. "Just head down the main channel and keep your eyes on the banks."

In the briefing over coffee, he'd told Terry that they had intel about enemy attempts to sink freighters coming up the channel into Saigon. They'd been successful before, and several ships sat on the bottom, only their scaffolding still above the surface to mark their watery graves. Fortunately so far, none had blocked the channel. But the enemy kept trying. They'd set up rocket launch sites on the riverbanks where they waited for the freighters. Today their job was to try to spot those launch sites.

There were a lot of little boats on the channel and on the tributaries going into it. The whole area was a giant mud flat from Saigon to Vung Tau, the city located at the mouth of the delta. Once it had been covered with giant nipa palm bushes and jungle trees, but they'd almost all been killed by defoliation chemicals. There were a few scraggily trees here and there, but it was mostly mud flats. Brush grew along the banks and that could hide some activity, but not much. The little boats were supposed to be fishermen and wood gatherers, but you could never tell. Sometimes the wood on the decks of the boats covered other cargo, like guns or rockets or VC.

On the good guys' side, they had their own boats on the river. There was a whole fleet of small navy jet boats that were armed to the teeth, which could maneuver in about three inches of water. The crews who manned them were often sitting ducks, but Terry and Don were their eyes in the sky. They would find the suspected enemy activity and then the boats would go in and investigate. The river boats were manned mainly by Seals, a dedicated group of professionals who knew how to fight—and often liked getting into the thick of the action.

"Take a turn up this channel," said Moss. "More cover here than on some of the others. Go up to 500 feet so we can look around."

Terry banked right into the small channel and started a climb. "Hand me your rifle," Don said.

"Spot something?"

"Not sure," he replied.

Moss had his rear side windows open. Terry passed the M-16 that he carried as a survival weapon over his shoulder to Don, who took it and rested it on the sill out his right window.

"Just don't hit the plane, okay?" Terry said with a mild chuckle.

"Right," said Don. "Swing around to the right—bank harder. See *that*?" he said. "Come around again." Terry banked more steeply. "See it? Hidden under the brush on the bank. That's pretty big for a woodcutter's boat. Hey—there's two of 'em." Excitement was building in his voice.

Terry saw them too. From the air he could make out the shapes of two larger than average boats, and they were obviously deliberately camouflaged. "See any VC?" he asked.

"No one around," answered Don. "Think you can hit one with a rocket?"

"I can sure try. What kind do you want?"

"Let's start with a Willie Pete so we have a good reference to work with. I'll get us some more firepower." He switched his radio to transmit, and he soon found one of his river boats in the area and a marine F-4 Phantom jet fully loaded with ordnance just a few miles north of Saigon.

"Cap'n Downey," he said formally, "you take the Fox Four and I'll take the river boat."

"Roger." Terry switched to the F-4's frequency and made contact. The F-4 would be on station in a few minutes. That would give Terry time to mark the target with a WP. With his left hand, he reached down and pulled the safety pin out of the trigger on the control stick. Then he reached up to the fire control panel and armed the right wing. All he had left to do was select which tube he wanted to fire and pull the trigger. He started his climb to a thousand feet as Don directed the patrol boat toward the target area.

"Hold it there," Terry heard him say to the boat below. "We're going to soften the area up a bit first." He switched to intercom. "Ready, Cap'n?" he asked.

No answer was necessary as Terry pushed the stick forward and pointed the nose at the target. His left hand went up to the fire control panel, and he flipped the switch to arm the outboard Willie Pete. At about 600 feet he pulled the trigger. They heard a "whoosh" as the rocket left the tube and sped toward the ground, leaving a white smoky trail as it went. Terry banked to the left and watched for the impact. There it was—a small plume of smoke rising from the mud flat about fifty yards from the target.

"Come back to the right," Don said, breaking his concentration. Terry banked back hard, standing the airplane nearly on its right wingtip, with the two of them looking out their right side windows straight down at the target area. Don shouldered the M-16 and started firing. He switched magazines and fired again.

He pulled the rifle back into the airplane and called the patrol boat. "Get in there and take a look, but be on guard," he warned.

They watched as the small patrol boat carefully worked its way toward the two beached wooden boats. The F-4 flew by overhead and checked out the marking smoke. "It's about fifty yards south of that smoke, Avenger Two-Five. You got it?" Terry asked him over the radio.

The F-4 pilot couldn't make out the target, but he could see the white smoke and the patrol boat, and from that he had a good idea of the target location.

They didn't hear it, but they both sure saw the flashes from the rifles as the area around the hidden boats came alive. The patrol boat had been ready and immediately fired back with its deck-mounted mini-gun, but not before they had taken several hits.

"Get outta there!" Moss shouted over the radio. It seemed forever before the patrol boat swung a tight circle and sped away upriver away from the target.

"I got the F-4 now," he said with authority, switching to the fighter's frequency. "Avenger Two-Five, make a couple of passes and ruin their day. Those guys shot up one of my boats."

"Roger, Moon River. I'll see what we can do," came the calm F-4 pilot's voice.

The F-4 made three passes to drop high-explosive ordnance. One was a direct hit. On his final pass, he laid an inferno of napalm right down the shore line on top of where the boats and the enemy had been. There was nothing left of the target but a watery hole surrounded by flame.

"Nothin' beats air superiority," said Don proudly.

"Another one for the good guys. Do we get a medal for this one?" Terry asked facetiously.

"Nah—just another day's work."

Terry reset his UHF radio back to company frequency just as Puck was making a call looking for him. "Aloft Three-Four, hang on the frequency a minute—the XO wants to talk to you."

Puck picked up the phone on his desk and rang the XO's office. "I've got Downey up on the UHF, Sir. He's standing by for your call back."

"Okay . . . well, just tell him to get back here right after the end of his mission and come see me first. No lollygagging around Saigon. Can you tell him that?"

"No problem, Sir. You want to hang on for a response?"

"Not necessary. Oh, and tell him it's nothing major, just need to see him. Don't want him getting all nervous or anything."

"Yes, Sir." Puck put down the phone and reached for the mike. "Aloft Three-Four, still there?"

"I'm not going anywhere if I can help it," Terry replied.

"The XO says come and see him when you get back to base and don't stop to play. He says it's nothing real important, just needs to see you."

A little acid crept into Terry's stomach. What would the XO want to see him about? "Roger, Aloft Base. I understand."

They flew to Vung Tau for lunch at the Officers' Mess and had an uneventful afternoon. He shot off his remaining rockets so that he wouldn't return to base with any evidence of broken rules. *Maybe that's it—the XO heard about the illegal rockets*, he thought.

"Don," he said, "you don't talk about the HE rockets to anyone, do you?"

"Hell no. What would I do that for? Why do you think I ask for you and Armanski? I sure as hell don't want a pilot like Mile High Milford. Hell, I can hardly get him below 3,000 feet. And he won't even fire the WPs."

It was little comfort. Someone else could have finked. He wouldn't even put it past Milford.

Corporal Deaver was waiting for them as they taxied into the FAC ramp at Tan Son Nhut. The Jeep was polished and shined. Don got in and turned to Terry. "See, I knew he could do it. Ya just gotta be firm. Smells funny though." They both laughed. Terry went back to his airplane for the flight back to Phu Loi. As Don drove off down the ramp and around the corner, he was yelling at Deaver the whole time. Marines seem to only have one tone of voice.

Chapter 16

Ski was intentionally keeping Terry out of his plan's inner circle. Pop had told him that the fewer the people involved, the better the chance of success. Ski had gone to him in confidence for some ideas, and it just had struck a cord with Pop. He was really an old softy at heart. He often said that the receiving is in the giving, and that was probably why he'd adopted the orphanage as a target of his generosity.

Ski knew he would eventually have to tell his friend all the details, but for now he just avoided the subject and let him think he was working on an adoption process. He visited the orphanage as often as time allowed between missions, working to build trust and friendship with his chosen "son." Each time he visited he taught him a new English word and he encouraged the nuns to help him by repeating it to him after he had left. It would break his heart if he couldn't make his plan work.

Pop had set a couple of his priorities aside to try to get his head around the task. There were so many details that had to be accomplished. If the adoption thing didn't work, and he was almost certain it wouldn't, then he had to fill in the blanks. He made a master list of what he needed:

One—a birth certificate. Just that one simple document would answer so many questions. He knew a doctor stationed at the hospital in Saigon. His dad was still a country doc in a small town in Iowa. Sometimes paperwork could be altered or created in a small town, and it just slipped through the cracks. He'd met the doctor at the O Club at the Air Force Mess in Saigon on one of his missions, and they'd struck up a conversation. The doc needed a particular OR instrument that the military didn't see fit to supply. They said he didn't need it. But with it, he could save lives in cases involving shrapnel wounds, and without it he was handicapped at best. Pop located one, traded for it, and hand-delivered it to him. The doctor was so grateful, he gave Pop his word, "anything you need that I can do, just let me know." Pop called in the favor. The paper work he needed would be waiting for him at the designated location when he arrived stateside.

Two—he needed to find a way out of the country and into the US without suspicion. That's where one of his original income stream plans came into play. But was he willing to risk a big chunk of his retirement income by adding additional out-of-the-box parameters? He'd only dwelt on the question for a moment or two. It was like he was being given the deal of the lifetime, and the money wasn't important. The universe had spoken, and he was obliged to answer.

Pop was not a religious man. He'd been raised Catholic but hadn't been to Mass for many, many years. He did, however, use his knowledge of the faith and its inner workings to garner favor with the local chaplain, who happened to be a priest. More deals, more favors—Pop was the master. But for some unknown reason, this touched his soul. It gave him a feeling of a greater purpose, and nothing was going to get in the way of success. And maybe the good deed would help absolve his soul for some of his less-righteous deeds.

Speaking of which, there was more than one Australian he'd owe an apology to if he ever met them. But there might be one or two that owed him as well, so maybe things evened up. Who knew for sure.

In Vietnam, the Aussies were like a breed apart, with a reputation as fierce fighters, and even better thieves. That made Pop a bit envious. They had a playful way about them, like everything was a game. They often seemed to be on a mission to best the US forces by doing things differently, but effectively. And if they needed something, like a Jeep or a tent, or a container full of rations, they just took them. They were masters at deception and tomfoolery. And except for the occasional supply sergeant who ended up missing various items from his inventory, they were universally loved. Well, maybe not universally. The NVA and VC took special pains to avoid their areas of operation because of how they "took care of business." Very seldom did the Aussies take a POW—and the enemy knew it.

But just like Zorro who enjoyed the favor of the common people and the ire of the bureaucrats, Aussies liked to let people know where they'd been. To them it was all a game. Whenever they stole something, they'd leave behind a calling card—a painted stencil of a kangaroo. It was like Zorro leaving his Z. Whenever a supply person saw the mark of the kangaroo, they could be sure that if they looked around, they'd find that something was missing.

Pop got the biggest kick out of that. He'd managed a couple of trades with them, and always said they were great to work with. It was all about honor among thieves and all that. But unknown to them, Pop also used their habits to his advantage. Sometimes when he misappropriated something, he knew it wouldn't be discovered for a long time. But in some cases, when he needed something in a hurry, he didn't always have the luxury to cover his tracks as well as he would have liked. He knew the missing item would be discovered quickly, and that wasn't healthy. In those cases, he left the mark of the Aussie, the stenciled kangaroo, and the blame automatically fell on them. God, they sure got blamed for a lot of stuff.

Chapter 17

Ski called Terry from Cam Rahn Bay to tell him he had a hop on an air force C-130 into Bien Hoa and to ask if he could pick him up at Major Snyder's office that night. Terry had an open schedule, so he reluctantly agreed. He really just needed to relax, what with all the stuff going on in his own life, but Ski was a good friend. He flew over in a Bird Dog at dusk, about seven-thirty in the evening. It was a short flight from Phu Loi, twenty minutes or so due east.

Big runways and American controllers made landing there easier than Tan Son Nhut. There was always a lot of traffic, but it was much more orderly. When Terry landed, he taxied into the maintenance area run by Major Snyder. He got out and headed toward the office. Ski had seen the Bird Dog taxi in and was just coming out on the ramp with his suitcase in hand to meet him.

"I hope you brought my helmet," said Ski. "I have a lot to talk to you about." He was still dressed in his Class A uniform, the beige TWs that had an open collar and short sleeves over dress slacks. He stowed his suitcase behind the rear seat, talking the whole time.

"How was the R&R?" Terry asked.

"Great!" he answered. "My wife is as excited as I am about Bobby."

As he climbed into the back seat and strapped on his seat belt, Terry handed him his flight helmet and said, "Ski, I hope you did more over there than just talk about Bobby."

"Well, there were a few other moments," he said with a grin as he pulled his helmet on, then plugged into the intercom system.

On the flight back to Phu Loi, he told Terry about his R&R in Hawaii—how Barbara had met him there, how great the civilian food was. They'd stayed in the Ilikai Hotel, right on Waikiki Beach. "You can imagine, there I am laying in bed at ten o'clock at night, and all of a sudden some idiot lights a string of firecrackers outside our room, just below our balcony. I rolled onto the floor and under the bed before Barbara even woke up. She reached out her hand, and when she realized I wasn't there, she thought I was in the bathroom or something. When she called my name and I answered from under the bed and told her I was looking for my pistol, she started laughing. Then we both laughed. Ever try to crawl out from under a bed when you're laughing? She asked me if this was some kind of weird R&R ritual. Well, those firecrackers sounded just like an AK-47—like Charlie coming through the concertina wire at the edge of the perimeter.

"Anyway, she checked with Immigration about adopting Bobby, and of course the fucking bureaucrats said no way!"

"That's too bad," Terry said. "I knew how much you were looking forward to it."

Ski responded with excitement in his voice. "No, that's okay That's what we figured would happen. The plan is still in effect. Barbara's brother is in on this now, and he's made some arrangements. It's still a go."

"Great!" Terry said, exasperated. "I hope you've got a miracle or two up your sleeve."

"I'll tell you about it tonight. Is Pop flying?"

"No, he's at home."

"Good—we'll have a meeting tonight, lay out the whole plan."

Terry hadn't heard the about a "whole plan" before, and it got his brain working. He just hoped it didn't involve him too much. He wanted to go back to the states still a captain if he could.

* * *

That night, they met in Terry's room. They had the old air conditioner turned on to make it a little more bearable. His roommates, Rick Partridge and Dave Newsome, were both flying. The fourth bunk had belonged to Billy before he was shot down and died. It was empty now. They would probably get a new guy in to fill it in a few days.

There were four of them at the meeting—Terry, Pop, Ski, and Hank Langford. Hank was the only guy in the company who openly professed to be a Christian. He knew a lot about the Bible. He was also a real brain, a graduate of Ole Miss, one of the nicest guys in the company. He was one of the project's planners and had given it the name—Operation Pussyfoot. He said it was something about former Vice President Spiro Agnew, and a speech he gave about his nemesis, the press, where he'd called them Pusillanimous Pussyfooters—whatever the hell that meant.

They put a card table between the bunks, and while Terry locked the door, Pop spread out a map on the table. "Pop," said Ski, "you lay it out. We'll make notes and ask questions."

"What's with the world map?" Terry said, sitting down on a bunk.

"I'll show you," said Pop. "We're here." He pointed to South Vietnam, roughly near the area of Phu Loi. "The exit route takes us from Phu Loi almost due east to the middle of the South China Sea. Then north, skirting the Philippines to the west. Then south and east of Taiwan, and on north to Okinawa—2,160 miles. Then down to Guam, 1,728 miles. Guam to Wake Island, 1,536 miles. Wake to Midway, a piece of cake—1,190 miles. Midway to Dutch Harbor, Alaska, and we're home free. Then over to Kenai. That's where we get the airplane repainted.

"The rest is simple. I already have the airplane sold for a nice chunk of change. Anyway, that's my business. Then we buy two tickets to Kansas, I drop off Bobby with Barbara, then head for Fort Eustis. If everything goes according to plan, I'll be able to report for my new duty ten days early if I want to. It's a nice cushion."

"Wait," Terry said. "What kind of airplane do you have that can fly that kind of distance? Even your Beaver can't make that. The OV-1 can refuel air to air, so you've hijacked a tanker, right?"

"No—and yes. My Beaver can make the trip," answered Pop calmly. "We have a 300-gallon auxiliary tank that I had built. It goes in the cargo compartment. I've been planning this for a lot longer then you think. Besides, I sold the Mohawk, remember?"

"Three hundred gallons?" Terry did a little arithmetic in his head, then said, "That's about 2,000 extra pounds of fuel. You'll be lucky to get off the ground."

"Oh, we'll make it. We just need a regular fuel load here at Phu Loi, and then we will fill up at Cam Ran Bay. That's an 11,000-foot runway, and that's all we need to get it airborne before we cross the ocean. The field at Guam is plenty long enough to let us get up and out. I'm just thankful for the nice tailwind I'll have going east bound."

"But . . . that means—"

Pop interrupted him. "Just sit still and hear me out. We'll do questions and strategy at the end."

Ski and Hank didn't seem concerned at all. They just listened and made notes as Pop outlined a flight in a single-engine Beaver to the other side of the world.

"That's about it. If we stay with the plan we mapped out, we'll be dealing mainly with the air force, and we don't need to worry about customs or big questions we can't answer," said Pop. "Coming in over the ADIZ will be the hardest part, but we'll be on a civilian flight plan by then. The customs guy at Dutch Harbor should be easy enough to handle. They'll just think we're another Anchorage training flight from Ft. Rich."

Terry was almost speechless. They were talking about flying almost halfway around the world, landing at some out-of-the-way places to avoid customs and international law, and smuggling a Vietnamese national into the US."

"By the way," said Pop. "I got something else in a trade with Major Snyder—a LORAN radio. Now this flight will be a piece of cake." As far as navigation equipment was concerned, the Beaver was now complete. The LORAN (Long Range Navigation) radio was what all the overseas aircraft used. It would give Pop his exact position in eight-digit coordinates nearly anyplace in the world.

"That's a real plan, Pop," Terry said, amazed.

"Yeah—it sure is," said Ski.

But Terry had to voice a real concern, though. "Pop, you can't make a trip like this alone."

"I can and I will," answered Pop. "I have my ways. And I'll get plenty of rest on my stopovers, trust me."

Terry knew better than to ask what that meant. Pop had something planned, and his plans usually worked. But he was still worried. "But the odds of it all coming together are pretty slim. Like, how are you going to explain your absence here? AWOL?"

The three looked at each, as if they had a shared secret. Pop said, "You know I rotate out next month, right? Well, I found a Red Cross guy that needs to get out, and they won't let him go. He's going to wear my uniform and take the big bird out riding in my seat. Then I'll be free to go my own way. It's not like they can call him AWOL. He's just going to quit his job when he gets stateside, and not tell anyone how he got there."

Terry scratched his head and looked at the map, then looked at the three planners. Armanski looked like the cat that had swallowed the canary. All smiles.

"I hate to play the part of the Devil's advocate," said Terry skeptically, "but how are you going to deal with having an illegal alien living in your home?"

"Pop, you want to take that one?" said Ski.

"We thought of that," said Pop matter-of-factly. " I arranged for a birth certificate that makes Barbara the mother."

"But—"

"Just listen. He's about five, maybe six, according to the best information the nuns can dig up. So Barbara had to give birth before she was married to Ski. And the "father" was oriental—and, by the way, deceased. Any more questions?"

Terry's head was practically spinning. "So how long have you been working on all this, and why have I been left out of the loop?"

"Time just wasn't right yet. Now it is," said Hank.

"Okay," Terry said. "You know you can count on me. What do you want me to do?"

"Terry," said Hank, "you're on R&R next week. We need you to make some phone calls. You know we can't call from here, and the mail is too slow and it could be read by the wrong people. Here"—he handed him an envelope—"a list of things to get done. They won't take long, but each one is important. The phone numbers are in there too. Ski put in some extra cash to pay for the long distance charges. If you have any left, have a drink on us."

"I'll do my best," said Terry.

The meeting didn't last long after that. They spent a little time going over the list and explaining the sequence of events, and how each one had to fall in place.

After the others departed, Terry lay back on his bunk and thought about Bobby. A little boy on a trip like that? And with crusty old Pop—alone? Good thing Pop liked kids. Good thing Bobby liked Pop. He's too young to understand the potential danger, and he'd be flying slower than Lindberg's *Spirit of Saint Louis*. Well, it was their only shot. He guessed it was worth a try.

Chapter 18

A Bird Dog with full fuel and a pilot exceeded gross weight. If you added an observer and some rockets, you were really pushing it. But when they hung that stupid exploding CS gas canister on the left wing, it took nearly all of the 5,000 feet of the runway to get off the ground. And then you could only climb at about 200 feet a minute. They were used to getting off the ground in under 800 feet and climbing at about a thousand feet a minute. But that extra 350 pounds hanging under the left wing, with a front surface that was flat to the wind, made the little airplane barely flyable. It was as if HQ thought that military orders could supersede the laws of physics. It sure put the pilot who had to fly that mission out on the edge.

They'd discontinued using the Beaver for mortar watch and had put the gas on the Bird Dog. By the time they got home after nearly four hours of flying and with the fuel tanks nearly empty, the airplane was just about down to maximum gross weight. But the left wing, where the canister hung, was sure heavy. The control stick had to be held over center to the right just to keep the wings level. Other than that, the mission was just like he'd done it in the Beaver.

Terry flew up and down Charlie Corridor for three-and-a-half hours looking for mortar flashes. He had no observer, but this out-of-trim plane kept him awake. It was still boring. He spent Christmas Eve and Christmas night *and* New Years Eve flying up and down Charlie Corridor in that first year. It was about ten minutes one way and ten back. He'd been warned to get up to 10,000 feet by midnight on New Years Eve and stay there—for good reason. He was listening to the countdown on AFVN on his ADF radio when, at the stroke of midnight, tracers suddenly shot up from the ground and filled the skies as every soldier—Vietnamese and American—fired rounds into the air to mark the beginning of a new year. It lasted for several minutes.

"Guard" frequency came alive with New Year's greetings from one company to another, from one headquarters to another. There was even a clear solid voice with a solid Harvard accent that claimed to be a North Vietnamese regular who had attended college in the US, who wished all American service men a Happy New Year. There was silence for a while after that one, and after a short while somebody came on frequency and said "Get off guard," meaning "clear the frequency for emergencies." The chatter pretty much stopped after that.

Before long, 0100 hours came and went. Then something funny happened. Bill Saunders, the pilot in Bravo Corridor, on the other side of the city, noticed an airplane coming into the Saigon zone. It was flying in slow circles to the left and holding about the same altitude. He called Terry on company frequency and said, "Terry, meet me on plus five," which meant go up point five on their frequency so headquarters, who monitored all transmissions, couldn't hear them.

Terry switched his transceiver. "Bill," he called, "What's goin' on?"

"'Look out there to the northeast. See the lights of that airplane circling out there?"

Terry turned his airplane and pointed the nose to the northeast. He spotted the red and green lights off in the distance. "I see it," he radioed back. "Could that be the ghost airplane they talk about, the one that comes into the corridors and then vanishes?"

"No, don't think so. I have an idea," said Saunders.

"I'll bet that's Ski. He has the Lerps northeast of Bien Hoa tonight, doesn't he?"

Terry had talked to Ski on the flight line. He was going to take off about a half hour before him for Lerp cover. "That's right," Terry radioed, "but he should be at least fifty miles north of here."

"Right," said Saunders, "but remember where the wind is blowing from—from the northeast at thirty knots, right? He's asleep, and the wind has blown him down here without him knowing it. I'm going to try to raise him on company freque."

They both switched back to company frequency. Terry heard Saunders call for him repeatedly. Nothing happened. The plane continued to make its lazy circles, and it kept getting closer and closer to Saigon. The two RAC pilots were growing more and more concerned—not just that he was out of his AO, but that given how long he'd been up and how far he'd drifted, he could have been asleep for nearly two hours, the maximum on one tank. It he didn't wake up and switch, the tank he was on might run dry and cause the engine to stop, and he might not get it restarted. He was at about 6,000 feet, but that's not much without a running engine—and being night it would be hard to find a good landing spot to glide to.

Saunders called again. "You stupid Pollack, Ski—get it in gear." He was practically yelling. Finally the plane straightened out. "Well, it's about time, Ski," he radioed.

No answer. They watched as the plane seemed to bank one way and then the other, as if he were getting his bearings. Ski had flown Charlie Corridor and Saigon enough to recognize it easily. It was the largest, most lit-up place in the country. He probably just couldn't believe what he was seeing. Then the airplane turned north and flew off. Saunders tried to call him a couple more times, but got no answer.

Terry wondered what Control back at HQ thought about this strange conversation. Pilots often carried on conversations from their various locations wherever they happened to be all over their operations areas within III Corps. Who knew what the company radio monitors thought? They had probably heard stranger conversations.

Back on the ground the next day, Saunders went to Armanski's room to find out what had happened. Ski denied the whole thing. He was sharp. Nobody could prove he wasn't right where he was supposed to be that night. He didn't really have anything to worry about though, because neither Bill or Terry would ever tell anyone about it—and if they did, they wouldn't say who the pilot was. Anyway, most of them had been guilty of a catnap once in a while. Eventually it would provide a good laugh and join the list of tales that became part of the company's folklore.

Ski never admitted what had happened. But after that, he seemed to look out for Saunders whenever he could, as if he was doing him a favor in return for something. They became good friends because of it. It was the only time Terry had ever heard Bill call anyone a Polack. It's probably the only time Ski heard it and didn't take a poke at the guy who said it.

Chapter 19

About a month after Terry got back from R&R in Hawaii, he got a letter from his dad. In it he said that Terry's Uncle Emery was going to Saigon and would be there on the tenth. He said that Terry should try to see him if he could. It was the ninth. Typical mail service. He was scheduled to fly tomorrow, but he switched with Rick Parmeter. He flew over to Lam Son and talked to his friend, Captain Mike Laramie.

Lam Son was an RVN support field. In order to fly there, you had to ask the tower at Phu Loi for permission to take off and land at the same time. The same tower controlled both airfields. All a pilot needed to do was take off and climb to about 200 feet, pull back power, bank left, round out, and land. That was how close the runways were. But both were surrounded by their own barbed wire and mines, so you couldn't just taxi over from one to the other.

Mike agreed to drive into Saigon with Terry, who picked him up the next day in the company Jeep out in front of the gate at Lam Son. Terry knew why his dad wanted him to see his uncle. Uncle Emery was a retired navy chaplain, had served in the South Pacific during WWII, and had reached the rank of commander. He now served as a missions director for a Christian world outreach organization. They were sending him to Vietnam to check out the situation with the people at a mission they sponsored there. What were the needs? How could they help?

Mike knew Terry was pretty angry with life in general. R&R was not what it was supposed to be. He'd had a major fight with his wife, and they hadn't parted on the best of terms—not that things were so great before. His dad had told him in several letters that there were problems back home. Terry hoped R&R would sort them out. After his wife had returned to the states, she'd taken off to Appleton, Wisconsin, with some other guy, and she wouldn't even write to him.

As they drove along the narrow winding roads that led through the delta to Saigon, Terry asked Mike a lot of questions. Mike didn't have a lot of answers. Mike was in Vietnam because it seemed he got along better with his wife when they had these periods of separation. So he was just fine. Terry had only gotten married about eight months before he got orders to Vietnam. They barely knew each other. They surely didn't know each other well enough to be like Mike and his wife, Melissa. As they drove, Terry's anger mounted. He took his .45 out of his shoulder holster and pointed it at people as they drove through traffic, weaving in and out of tiny cars and scooters. The Vietnamese on their Honda motor scooters would see the pistol and veer off the road. Terry would hear loud gibberish hurled at them. He could only guess what they were saying. Terry thought out loud, "Isn't it amazing how they can get five people on one little motor scooter? I guess it's 'cause together they still weigh less than two fully grown Americans."

When they got to Saigon, the roads were crowded with bicycles and scooters—three-wheeled bicycles and motorized cabs, scooters, all racing around. An army Jeep was huge among all the little vehicles crowding the narrow avenues. It took about an hour to find the hotel where Terry's Uncle Emery was staying. It was now noon, and they couldn't stay very long because they had to be back in Phu Loi by dark or be locked out of the compound. Not a happy thought.

Mike checked at the desk while Terry looked around. He found his uncle drinking a cup of tea at a table in a little vine-covered patio area, just off the lobby. Terry waved to Mike, and he came over to join them. Emery was not a tall man, but he was built tough, with strong arms and upper body, and a very firm hand shake. Actually, he was built a lot like Mike. His square jaw said that this was a man who got right down to business. But Terry knew him as one of the world's great pranksters. He'd met Richard Nixon before he'd become president, and he'd only spoken with him for a minute or two. Evidently Nixon had been impressed with him, though. Emery told a story about how a few years later he'd heard then-President Nixon was to be speaking at a banquet near Emery's home in Nashville. He found a way into the banquet hall through the kitchen and down a back hall, and confronted the president as he was coming through a rear entryway with a secret service man at each elbow. The startled secret service men had moved to grab him, but when the president called Emery by name, they halted. He told the president how much he appreciated him and how he was praying for him. This seemed to really impress Mr. Nixon, who thanked him, shook his hand, and went on down the hall, secret service men in tow. Emery always told that story to show how important it was to remember people's names. It is a trait good politicians share.

Even husky Mike, the tattooed motorcycle rider, winced a little bit when Terry introduced them and he shook Commander Emery Downey's hand. Emery remarked that Mike must have been in the navy. Mike said he was and asked how he knew. He pointed to the tattoo of the naked woman on Mike's left forearm, and they both laughed. "Easy enough to tell," Emery said with a grin, "I guess I was just in the navy too long myself."

"Actually," said Mike, "navy and marines. Terry told me that you're retired."

"Yes—still have the rank though. Reserves." He turned to Terry. "Time for some serious talk, Nephew. Your dad's real worried. How are you feeling?"

"I'm fine, Sir—really." Terry answered. Mike rolled his eyes.

"If nearly shooting three nationals on the road to get here is fine, then I guess you're fine," said Mike. "It was just a good thing I was driving."

"Sit down," said Uncle Emery. "Want something to drink?"

"Only if they have some ice," said Mike. "I can't stand warm Coke."

Emery signaled the waiter and ordered two Cokes with ice, which turned out to be an ordeal. When the waiter left, he said, "I guess they understand tea better. It's a lot easier to order that."

He turned and looked Terry straight in the eye. Terry couldn't turn away. "Terry," he said, "I know things are a little rough right now. But you only have, what—five months more to go, and then you're on your way home?" His steel blue-gray eyes locked in on him. "You need to focus on the job. Take care of it now. Deal with the rest when you get home. You can't deal with it while you're here."

Terry started to speak but Emery wouldn't let him. "The best advice I can give you is, find something in this war that's worthwhile and do it. Use it to get your mind off of yourself and onto other people. Your company have any goodwill projects?"

Terry's mind flashed. His Uncle Emery saw it in his eyes, and it caught him by surprise. The corner of Terry's mouth curled a little. "'I do have a project I've been working on, and you may be just the guy to help." Terry turned and looked at Mike. "Mike, you gotta forget everything you hear. Promise?"

"So what's new? I forget most of what you say as a matter of course," said Mike.

"Uncle Emery, forget about my problems. I have too much of an upbeat personality to let this get the best of me. It hurts, but the days are passing. It'll get better. Let me tell you about Project Pussyfoot. Tell me what you think."

Terry outlined the basics of the plan as Mike and Emery listened carefully. Emery could tell by Terry's enthusiasm that

Recon Airplane Company: III Corps, Vietnam

he was serious. Emery had what some called "Brass." It was what let him sneak up on the President of the United States just to say hi. It was what had helped get him promoted to commander. And it also allowed him to bend military regs once in a while.

As he was wrapping up his narrative, Terry asked his uncle if he might look into handling some "paperwork" issues to help get a five-year-old into the US. Mike broke in and warned that they would have to head back soon.

Emery sensed Terry's excitement about this humanitarian mission and encouraged him to proceed, but carefully. He said he'd look into what he could do and get back to him. Finally, he urged him to pray. *What else should I expect from a chaplain?* Terry thought.

Emery saw his look and admonished him gently. "God can make a big difference. He always has for me. Give Him a chance, Terry."

Then he prayed for them. Terry gave him a hug and shook his hand, then he and Mike went back to find the Jeep. Mike got in, unlocked the big padlock and chain that he'd put on the steering wheel, and they headed back to Phu Loi.

On the drive back, they talked about the big plan. Mike was worried for Terry and the others, all his friends. "I don't know how Pop's going to pull off that Beaver flight," he said. "I for one think he's a little crazy. For one thing, he's too old."

"You should hear him talk about it, Mike. He's like a kid. The only thing that pisses him off is that when he pulls it off, there'll only be a handful of people who'll know that he did it, and he'll be breaking a few world records when he does it."

"You talk like it is going to work," said Mike. "Well, good luck with that."

* * *

Back at the orphanage, the sisters were preparing the evening meal. The children were just coming in from playtime and cleaning up in the big basin they used for washing hands and faces. Sister Ellen poured a fresh pitcher of water into the basin and kept the line of children moving forward, handing each a towel as they finished.

Bobby, as they were all calling him now, took his towel and went over to a wooden chair next to the big stone fireplace. A couple of others about his age came and sat on the floor near him. They were chattering in Vietnamese.

What does a boy of five or six think about? The sisters had gently told him that he wouldn't see his mother again. They'd been north to the village where he had lived, and had gathered a lot of background on the unusual French-speaking boy. They heard about his father and mother from the villagers, so now they knew he was all alone—except for the sisters and the army guys who came by once in a while with stuff for the orphanage. He kind of liked the one guy who always brought him something special, but he really missed his own father. Whenever he thought of him, he was filled with sadness. Then he would think of his mother and that hurt worse.

But the nuns were so nice, and they spoke his special language—just like his parents. That always cheered him up. It made him feel a little like he was with relatives who cared for him.

A few days ago, the sisters had sat them all down in the big hall. They did this every few months, and it was important—especially for the new kids. They explained as best they could about the war and the soldiers. Then they'd tell them about the special hiding places that had been created in the compound and in the old plantation building, just in case the wrong soldiers came by to loot, or try to recruit the older children. They were also told about the tunnel that led to the edge of the river, where they could escape and run into the jungle to hide. It was a good plan if they were not caught by surprise. So far, they hadn't had to activate the evacuation plan.

Bobby listened. It was a lot like the run-away games his mother had taught him. Run as fast as you can, get a long way away, and then hide and be very quiet. It had been quite awhile since he'd thought of his last escape. He put his hand on his head and felt the scar from the gash that a VC rifle butt had put there. The other kids were making fun and joking about who would be first in the tunnel. Bobby just listened.

Chapter 20

"Ski, listen to me," said Pop, sounding almost angry, "I only have a two-day window of opportunity. If I don't leave by tomorrow at 0600, the whole plan will fall through. I already lost my seat home to that Red Cross guy. He left yesterday. Everybody here thinks I'm gone."

"But the whole reason for the flight is to get Bobby out, remember?" pleaded Ski.

"Not in the beginning. He was just an add-on, but I understand your frustration," said Pop sympathetically. "But he's gone, and you got about two chances of finding him—slim and none." Pop put his arm around Ski's shoulder and gave him a gentle hug.

Ski hung his head.

"Let's try going up to the orphanage one more time. Maybe they have some news," said Terry.

Ski looked at Terry with hope in his eyes.

Pop just rolled his eyes and said, "Terry! We've been there six times in the last three days. When the VC hit the place, everyone scattered. It's no telling where they are by now. It's lucky they left the nuns alive. There's nothing we can do."

"Come on, Ski—one more try. You and me. We'll go have a look," said Terry.

Pop didn't like it. He clearly thought it was a waste of time, and now he should be focused on just getting himself out and following the rest of the plan. But they'd come this far together. That's what this brotherhood was all about, wasn't it? "All right," he said, "one more try."

"One more thing," said Terry. "Bring all the guns we can muster—I have an idea. And see if you can get Langford to come along. Meet me back here at the Beaver in a half hour."

"Right," answered Ski. Then he turned and took off at a run toward the Officers' Quarters.

* * *

The Beaver was sitting in the transient parking area at Phu Loi, well away from the company area. Everyone thought Pop had taken a normal "big bird" flight out of the country. As of yesterday, he was company history. Instead, he'd put a bedroll in the Beaver and spent the night in the cargo compartment. He'd planned to leave the following day, just as soon as they picked up Bobby from the orphanage. But that night, the VC had pulled a raid on the orphanage and had taken every boy of about ten years and older for service in their noble cause. The rest had run off into the jungle or gone into their special hiding places. The nuns had managed to find some of the younger ones and bring them back. But Bobby was gone. They hoped he'd taken the tunnel and disappeared into the safety of the jungle. But he was big for his age. They hoped that he was not taken by the VC as a new recruit.

Pop's dilemma was real. If he didn't get back to the states and check into his duty station on time, he'd be AWOL, and the whole scheme might unravel. That would mean court-martial for him and maybe for some of the Pussyfoot planners as well. It could also red flag his other activities. With the Red Cross guy flying home in Pop's seat, the plan had to go forward, with or without Bobby. And then there were the tail winds. They were really in his favor right now, and he just couldn't ignore the extra thirty-five knots. It was like an insurance policy.

* * *

Terry drove the Jeep and Langford rode shotgun. Pop and Ski were in the back seats. They all had an M-16 at the ready and a pistol on their hip—or in a shoulder holster, where Terry kept his .45, concealed under his shirt. Langford had an M-79 grenade launcher with shotgun loads for good measure.

When they drove into the orphanage courtyard, no one ran out to greet them. There were no children playing. Ski got out of the Jeep and started toward the main door. The rest of them took up defensive positions around the Jeep. No telling who was here these days. As Ski approached the entrance, the door began to open, and he dropped to one knee with the M-16 at the ready. Out came Sister Carol. Ski stood up and slung the M-16 over his shoulder.

"Hello, Sister—were back again," he said. "Any news on Bobby?"

Sister Carol walked up to Ski and put her arm around him. In a quiet voice she said, "I'm sorry, Steve—we can't find him. Sister Ellen went into the village this morning to try to find some of the kids. She only found one. The villagers are real scared there too. They lost some of their children to the VC the same night."

Pop came up to them as they were talking. He could tell by Ski's bowed head that the news wasn't good. "Come on," he said, "that's it." He took Ski by the arm and started to escort him back to the Jeep. He took a couple of steps and turned back to Sister Carol. "Pray for us, please. Terry wants to go into the village and have a look around. If we see Sister Ellen, we'll give her a ride home."

They drove out of the compound and headed north. The village was only about four miles away, but it was reportedly a VC staging area. It was Terry's idea, but it was scary. Anything could happen. One voice inside him said there was a good reason for all this, but another said they could be driving into deep shit. After all, they were just a bunch of pilots, not ground pounders.

They'd never been to the village before. As they got close, Terry slowed the Jeep, and they all checked their weapons. Langford loaded the M-79 and cocked it over his right arm like he was out pheasant hunting in Alabama. The village consisted of just a couple dozen hooches, small buildings built out of spare boxes, twigs, and lumber from other places that had been blown up or fallen down. There was also a small outdoor market. Animals of various kinds wandered about the streets and in and out of the houses.

They stopped the Jeep at the edge of the village and got out, all facing in different direction, rifles at the ready. No sooner did the villagers notice them than they heard the mama-san's shrill screams as they gathered up their children and ran for cover. They hadn't intended to create such a stir, but soldiers never meant good to these people. All they ever did was destroy, whoever they were, whichever side they were on. All the villagers wanted was to be left alone, grow their rice and vegetables, and live in peace. But they hadn't known peace for decades.

They walked carefully into the village. Pop walked behind and with his back to the group so that he could keep an eye on the way they'd come. One old man was sitting outside his hooch, chewing on some betelnut. Their presence didn't seem to bother him a bit. Pop went over to him. "We looking for boy," said Pop as he bent over and motioned with his hands to try to describe a small child. The old man looked at Pop with uncaring eyes. "*Tumwee, dinkedow*" was his reply.

Pop knew enough Vietnamese to know that the old man thought he was crazy to be there. He straightened up. "Let's look around, boys. But be careful."

They started to walk through the village. No one seemed to understand them. Ski remembered that he had a picture of Bobby and began showing it to the villagers. After about ten minutes, the villagers were more at ease. They realized that the soldiers were not there on some kind of raid. They began to come up to them, look at Ski's picture, and shake their heads. The little children would come up slowly and touch one of them, then run back to Mama-san.

They stayed in the village about thirty minutes or so, asking questions as best they could with the few Vietnamese words they knew, and lots of sign language. Terry saw Pop motion to Ski, and their eyes met. Ski knew it was a lost cause.

"Time to go home, guys," said Ski. "Nothing more we can do here." He was close to tears.

They brought their rifles back to the ready and headed for the Jeep. Several of the villagers followed them. One toothless old woman hit Ski on the leg and held out her hand in the universal language of begging. Ski reached into his pocket, found a few coins to give her, and walked on. It was amusing to watch her smile.

The soldiers waved to the villagers as Terry turned the Jeep around. They all got in and headed back toward the south toward Phu Loi, leaving a trail of dust behind them.

Just as they were driving off, there was a commotion at the other end of the village. A nun came running into town with a little boy running alongside, holding onto her hand. She waved at them.

But the sound of the engine and exhaust of the noisy Jeep drowned out the yells that were now well behind them. Ski stared straight ahead, and none of them looked back. They were a bit relieved to be heading back to the safety of the compound, but they were disappointed as well. Ski's head was down for the whole ride.

* * *

The next morning, Ski and Terry watched as Pop made his take-off run in the overloaded Beaver. When he got off the ground—barely—and cleared the fence at the end of the runway, it made him think "Just like Lindberg," and he breathed a sigh of relief. He was concerned about Pop's long ocean crossing. Once in the air, Pop made a gentle bank to the west, and they watched as he disappeared into the morning sky. If he made it, it would be another addition to the Danforth legend. If he didn't, no one would probably ever know what really happened.

Ski looked at Terry, and his eyes filled with tears. He looked away. "It was a great dream, Ski," Terry whispered quietly.

About three hours later that same day, while Terry was getting his mission orders from Puck in the company operations bunker, there was a call from the gate guard at the compound entrance. "Please find Captain Armanski and send him down to the gate. There's a nun who wants to see him." Puck repeated the call out loud. "Some guy down at the main gate wants to see Ski about a nun." Then he added, "I better call the CO and tell him."

"No!" Terry said quickly. "I'll get Ski and go see what it is. No need to bother the old man."

Terry ran up the stairs and over to the officers hooches. When he ran into the room, Ski was lying on his bed, looking up at the ceiling.

"Ski!" he said excitedly. "One of the sisters is at the main gate and wants to see you."

He sat straight up. "Here? Now?"

"Yeah, now!" Terry answered. "Let's go."

When they got to the gate, there was sister Ellen with a big smile on her face. "We found him, we found him," she said excitedly.

They looked at each other and motioned for her to walk across the road with them. This was no place to discuss this situation. The guards were already looking at them like they were nuts. Damned MPs—suspicious of everything.

"Listen, Sister," said Ski, "I'm glad you found him, but it's too late. Pop took off three hours ago. There's no way to get him back." Ski looked at Terry and nearly broke down again. Sister Ellen told how they had just missed her at the village. Now Ski was beside himself.

"Look, Terry. Let's try to reach Pop on the UHF. There's still a chance."

Ski turned to the nun. "Where's Bobby now?" he asked impatiently.

Sister Ellen motioned up the road to where a small motor scooter was sitting with a young Vietnamese man standing alongside, and he could see a small boy sitting on the seat, pretending to be driving. He could just hear him going "Brrrm, brrrm," as he twisted the throttle.

"It's worth a try," Terry said. "Ski, go get a Jeep and get the boy inside the compound. I'll try to raise Pop. Wait—on second thought. He couldn't get back here for another three hours anyway." He turned to the nun. "Sister, take the boy and go back to the orphanage. Meet us back here in about two hours."

Ski waved to Bobby and Bobby waved back. Terry grabbed Ski by the shirtsleeve and pulled him into the compound. "We've got no time to lose. He's probably out of range already."

They ran back to the company area and almost flew down the stairs into the operations room. "Puck, we gotta use the UHF for a few minutes. Get lost."

"Not on your life," he answered. "I have to stay here. It's my job."

"All right, stay—but forget what you hear, okay?"

"How much is it worth," said the clerk.

"How about a two-day R&R to Vung Tao?" Terry said, offering his favorite bargaining chip.

"Deal. What frequency you need?" he said with a big smile.

"Two-forty point four," said Ski, "and give me the mike."

Puck dialed in the frequency and Ski began his call. "Pussyfoot, Pussyfoot, this is Pussyfoot One, do you read?"

"Ah what a tangled web we weave, when first we practice to deceive," said Puck.

"Shut up," said Terry and Ski in unison.

They waited. No answer. He tried again. "Pussyfoot, Pussyfoot, this is Pussyfoot One, do you read?" Still no answer. Ski turned to Puck, "What's the best range you've ever gotten out of this box?"

"Sometimes, late at night I've been able to talk to Four Corps."

"That's only a couple hundred miles. He's got to be better than 300 out. We'll never get him with this one."

"Who are you talking about?" said Puck.

"None of your *business*, Shakespeare. I told you to forget this, right?" said Terry.

"No need to get nasty." said Puck, his feelings hurt.

The thought hit them both at the same time and they looked at each other and said together, "The Beaver!" The company Beaver, the *real* one, had a great UHF radio. If they got off the ground and a couple thousand feet or more up, they'd have a good chance of making contact.

Ski turned to Puck. "Not a word of this to anyone!" Puck nodded, and the two co-conspirators ran back up the stairs and headed for the flight line.

There was the Beaver, tied down in its assigned revetment, as always. "You preflight, I'll check with the line chief."

While Ski ran over to the aircraft to untie the wings and tail and do a routine check—oil, fuel—Terry hurried over to the line shack and found the sergeant in charge. "Anything scheduled for the Beaver for the next hour?" he asked quickly.

The sergeant put down the magazine he was reading and looked up at the schedule board. "Not that I know of," he replied. "Goin' somewhere?"

"No, just want to do a test flight. We'll be back in less than an hour."

Terry got to the airplane just as Ski was finishing the hasty preflight. "I'll fly, you work the radios," Terry said as he climbed into the pilot's seat. Ski got into the copilots seat and they both strapped in. Terry gave it a couple pumps on the engine primer, brought the wobble pump up to pressure, and engaged the starter. It began to wind up, louder and faster, until it was at that pitch every Beaver pilot knew. He hit the engage switch and the propeller started to turn. One, two, three revolutions, and he engaged the mag switch. He heard the loud pop-sputter-sputter as the radial engine came to life. Blue smoke poured out the exhaust as the engine cleared the residual oil that had drained into the bottom cylinders.

Moving as quickly as they could, they taxied off the flight line and called for clearance to take off. No run-up today. No time. They would have to believe that the Beaver would forgive them this time, as it had so many times before.

It took about fifteen minutes to get off and up to 2,000 feet. Terry maintained a constant climb attitude and Ski started making his calls to Pussyfoot. After another fifteen minutes they reached 10,000 feet and Ski heard nothing. He was becoming more frantic as his frustration built. Then he heard it. "Pussyfoot One, this is Pussyfoot. Go ahead."

"Pop, can you hear me?" said Ski in a near panic voice.

"Roger, hear you weak but clear," came the reply.

Ski looked at Terry with huge relief. He practically shouted with joy into the microphone. "Pop, we got him. We got the Pussyfoot kid."

Silence.

"Pop, do you hear me?"

"I hear you," said Pop. "What do you want me to do?"

"Come back and get him, please," Ski begged expecting a positive response.

Silence. Then, "Listen, Ski. I'm point of no return. Just talking to you now they could get a lock on me. I'd never make it back. I'll clear the next border in under an hour. I can't come back."

Inside the long-range Beaver, Pop felt like his heart would burst. He knew how much this meant to Ski, to the boy—and to himself. He thought hard. Was there a way? He could come back in through Phan Rang, but he'd made no arrangements there, and there was a chance he'd be caught and inspected. He was devastated. The logic was overwhelming. There was no way to return. There was nothing more to say. All he could do now was apply himself to the task at hand.

In the other Beaver, Ski looked over at Terry. What a day. What a past couple of days. Close, but no cigar. His face told the whole story.

Terry switched to his mike and called Pop on the UHF. "Pussyfoot, no need to answer. Have a good flight. Good luck. See you back home. And thanks for trying. Pussyfoot One, out."

Chapter 21

Terry left Ski in his room. Ski had gotten out his stationary and was trying to figure out what to write home to Barbara. Pop was going to call her as soon as he got stateside, but a letter from him would help ease the pain, a little. Terry, meanwhile, had to get to Dau Tieng and defend the old Michelin rubber plantation yet again. He'd flown that mission before. Not much to it.

When Terry landed, he taxied directly to the refueling point. It was just a wide spot off the side of the runway. There were fueling bladders, larger rubber containers that held various kinds of fuel for the aircraft that flew in and out of Dau Tieng. He parked the airplane and put a chock under the right wheel. He methodically attached the grounding cable to the wing strut and went over to the small pump. He had to pull-start the one-cylinder engine like an old lawn mower. He wrapped the rope around the starter hook and gave it a yank. It took a couple of tries, and then it sputtered and came to life. He unhooked the fuel hose and nozzle from its post and, with the nozzle in one hand, he climbed up on the wing strut step. Balancing himself with one foot on the strut and the other on the fuselage step, he opened the fuel cap on the right wing and began to fill up the Bird Dog with AV gas.

About the time he was starting to fill the second tank, a Jeep drove up. It was Lt. Darlington. He'd flown as his observer here at Dau Tieng several times before. Always cool under pressure, he had a lot on the ball. He was wearing the normal jungle fatigues and had a .45 in a holster on his waist. He shut off the engine on his Jeep and came over to where Terry was working.

"How ya doing today, Captain?" he said with a chipper voice, yelling so that he could be heard over the sound of the pump motor. "Can I give you a hand with the hose?"

"Thanks," Terry answered. "I'm almost done. I'll hand it down to you."

He watched as Terry finished topping off the tank. It was standard procedure to always fill the tanks up. The airplanes were overweight regardless, but the pilots felt better with the insurance of as much fuel as they could squeeze in—just in case they had to fly to some other base, or stay on station longer than expected. He handed the hose and nozzle down to Darlington, who took it, hung it back on its hook, and shut off the pump.

"What's on the agenda for today?" Terry asked, making sure both fuel tank caps were secure before climbing down from the wing strut.

"Pretty much routine. We have an artillery adjustment to the south, and they want us to do a little scouting to the west over by the Razorbacks. But I have a special request for you."

"Shoot," Terry said as he opened the engine cowl to check the oil.

"Well, we have a new guy." He hesitated. "He's kind of a know-it–all." He paused again. "We want you to take him up this afternoon for a little—shall we say . . . orientation flight. He can do the artillery registration, and then you can do the recon over by the Razorbacks."

"That's fine," Terry said. "I've flown with most of you guys here one time or another. I'll show him the ropes."

"No—you don't understand. This guy has been telling us for a week how good he is. Everything anyone has done, he's done it better. You ever meet a guy like that?"

"Sure," Terry replied. "We have one just like that in our company—Capt. Newman. We call him "Nude" Newman. I'll tell you the story sometime. But what does all this have to do with me? Sounds like you want to pawn your problem child off on me so you can have a quiet afternoon."

"We have a little bet going with him that he can't survive the kind of flying we do here without upchucking. Remember that time you did that split "S" with me and I nearly lost it?"

"Say no more. But you get someone to clean up the airplane when I get back."

"All *right*!" Darlington said excitedly.

Terry opened the cockpit door, grabbed the cross bar in front of the windshield, and swung himself up and into the pilot's seat. "You gonna pick me up at the revetment, or am I gonna hafta walk?"

"I'll see you there," Darlington replied. He got in his Jeep and headed for the parking area at the north end of the airfield. Terry started up the Bird Dog and checked the runway for other traffic, then taxied down to the parking area. There was no tower to talk to here in this out-of-the-way place. A pilot just had to keep a close eye out on what was going on and stay clear of other airborne and ground traffic on his own.

At Dau Tieng, as at most of the places that the pilots stayed, they parked the aircraft in revetments. They were large metal-sided, earth-filled, high-walled, protected bunkers that they could taxi into, and in case of a mortar attack, be protected from most of the enemy fire. Terry tied down the wings with the ropes that were in place in the revetment and got Lt. Darlington to help him switch out the rockets. The pilots who did that had an even better option here. Since he had eight tubes to work with, he loaded two with HE and two with flechette rockets—or "nails," as most everyone called them. This was a special rocket that, after firing, the warhead exploded like a small grenade after a couple of hundred yards. The explosion separated the secondary part of the warhead, which was composed of hundreds of little steel darts. They looked like the darts a person would play with, except they were smaller, about two inches long, and solid, with solid fins. As soon as they hit the air stream, they oriented themselves in the direction the rocket was fired and practically flew in a straight line toward the target. But instead of a small impact zone, they spread like bird-shot over fifty or sixty square yards.

Terry always loaded the rockets in the same order. The four remaining outboard tubes still had the marking rounds in place. That way he could still do his assigned mission, but if the right opportunity presented itself, he could do a little more. It was like having a backup plan. He always liked to keep his options open.

That afternoon, after the colonel's briefing, Lt. Darlington drove Terry and the new guy, Lt. Finch, along with one of the other regular observers, out to the revetment for the afternoon mission. They bid their "friend" and Terry farewell with a grin, and drove away. Terry gave Finch the standard briefing, which included "Keep your hands off of the controls," and they got in and fastened their seatbelts. Terry had to show him how to attach the shoulder harness and where the mike button was. He seemed confident enough, though.

Terry started the airplane and taxied to the warm-up area. After a brief run up, he taxied into place at the end of the runway and applied full power. The Bird Dog responded as always. As soon as they broke ground, Terry leveled off and held the plane about two feet off the runway as it continued to gain speed. When he reached the end of the runway, which was also the perimeter of the compound, he pulled the nose up hard and banked right. "You okay back there?" he called over the intercom.

"Just fine," came the reply, but Terry could tell Finch's voice was a little strained.

"Good. Tell me where you want me to go." He put the monkey on Finch's back for the navigation, even though he knew the area well. The guys wanted Terry to give him the full test, see how he could handle it, show him that he wasn't as good as he thought he was.

Amazingly enough, he directed Terry to the right area. They did the artillery adjustment, and he did a good job at it. Terry made some steep turns over the target to see how he would respond. He seemed to handle it well. Next stop, the Razorbacks.

The Razorbacks are a mountain range about fifteen miles west of Dau Tieng. It was great high ground. The US didn't have anyone up there, but they suspected Charlie did. Whenever the pilots had flown over it in the past, they'd seen some signs of past occupation, but nothing was going on while they were observing. The mountains were only about a thousand feet high, but the surrounding jungle was fairly flat, so you could see a good distance from up there. Anyone on top could certainly monitor activity at Dau Tieng. It was their job to take another look. It was Terry's personal job to make this new guy barf. He told him when they left that if he felt queasy to hang his head out the window. Terry just hoped he'd follow instructions.

Terry was over the mountains at about 5,000 feet. "See anything down there?" he asked.

"No, not yet," replied Finch.

"Well, keep looking." Finch's attention was focused on the ground as Terry rolled the Bird Dog upside-down and cut the throttle. It hung there for a couple seconds before the nose dropped and they began their rapid descent, headed straight for the ground. "Time for a little closer look," he said, trying to sound like this was just another standard maneuver.

He leveled off at about a hundred feet above the jungle floor at maximum speed, then headed straight for the wall of the mountain that rose up before him. He glanced out of the corner of his eye to see how Finch was doing. Finch was holding firmly to the window sills with both hands. He looked a little white. *So far so good*, thought Terry.

When it seemed that impact with the cliff was imminent, Terry pulled back on the control stick and flew almost straight up the side of the mountain. He pushed the nose over at the top, and they both felt their stomachs rise. Although Terry was used to it and prepared, the weightless feeling was still there. He glanced at Finch again. "Check out the top of this mountain. See anything?" He didn't get an answer. Another good sign. He leveled off and flew along the contour of the top of the mountain. It was a little like riding a roller coaster. As he came up the last gentle slope, he prepared for the coup de grace. He came flying along the bluff, knowing that he was coming to a sheer drop-off. As soon as he cleared the last part of the mountain below, he pushed the nose straight over and headed for the jungle floor again. "Keep your eyes open for Charlie," he said calmly.

As they neared the jungle canopy he pulled up again and banked right. "You think we could just fly straight for a while?" came a pathetic plea from Finch.

Terry immediately leveled off. "Problem?" he asked.

"No problem," Finch replied, sounding a little less wobbly. "I just want to get my bearings."

They landed about an hour later. As they taxied into the revetment, three of the regular FOs were there to greet them, all smiling expectantly. "Well Finch, how did it go?" Darlington asked.

"Great flight," said Finch. "Didn't find anything, though."

They looked at Terry and he looked back at them and shrugged his shoulders. Finch had come through it all with the contents of his stomach intact.

On the ride back to their company area, they told Terry that they had a late mortar watch that night. When they got out of the Jeep, they showed him to his bed in the deep bunker close to the operations shack. After dinner, he laid down to take a nap. Lt. Darlington woke him up at 2230 hours to tell him it was time to fly. They were in the air by 2300.

Uneventful. That was the word for most mortar watches. Just like Saigon, not much usually happened on mortar watch. But they'd been in the air for about two hours when they saw flashes of light, just like that night over Saigon, over to the east of the compound. Those were mortars, all right. Terry saw them first and pointed them out to Darlington, and he called them into base.

"Terry? Think you can hit 'em with HE?" said Darlington over the intercom.

"They're a way off, but it's worth a try," he answered.

Terry pointed the nose of the airplane straight at the flashes of light. They looked to be a little out of range, so he increased throttle to full power. The flashes continued. After about a minute he reached up and armed two HE rockets, pointed the nose at the flashes, and pulled the trigger. The rockets left the tubes with a flash of white hot light, and they watched them as they headed toward the enemy firing position. Terry leveled back off. He reached up and armed the two nails. After about another minute, he lowered the nose again and pointed it at the flashes in front of him. He pulled the trigger. Two more rockets sped from the Bird Dog's wings. They watched as they raced toward the ground. Then they saw another flash as the rockets reached their scatter point and the little darts came free and headed on their flight toward the target.

As they watched, there were no more flashes of light from the ground. The attack appeared to be over. Darlington radioed back to base, and they flew over the area trying to pin down the coordinates for the ground team that would go in the next morning to try to find the mortar site. The rest of the night was quiet.

* * *

The next day, while they were eating their evening meal in the officers' side of the mess hall, Terry saw Finch come in and look around. When he spotted Darlington and Terry, he came over to their table, pulled out a chair, and turned it around and straddled it. He put his crossed arms on the back of the chair and looked at them and said, "Well, you got their attention this time."

Darlington and Terry looked at each other, then back at Finch, questioningly.

"Okay, Lieutenant," Terry said, "spit it out."

"You guys haven't heard yet, have you?" He said with a little surprise.

"Heard what?" said Darlington with a bit of irritation.

Finch smiled. "To bad you can't claim this one, Sir. It was a good shot."

Finch could see Terry was getting upset. He'd put his knife and fork down and was now looking straight at him.

"Sorry, Sir," he said. "You guys nailed that mortar team last night," he chuckled. "Literally."

Terry was puzzled, and Finch went on.

"The patrol they sent out this morning found a six-man mortar team at the coordinates you reported last night. They were all dead. Little tiny holes in 'em. Except for one—he was nailed to a tree and just hanging there, held up by these little dart things."

He paused and held out his hand to show a flechette dart between his thumb and index finger.

"Well, that's the way to fight a war," Terry said. "I can't wait to tell the guys back at the company. They'll get a real kick out of it."

"By the way," said Finch, "the old man loves it. But if he writes it up, he knows you'll be in a heap of trouble. He's not even gonna talk to you about it. He says you should get a medal, but he knows your company policy about the rockets. Always WP, right?"

"Blast. That means I better keep my mouth shut back home too," said Terry.

Darlington smiled. "Six enemy KIA. Pretty good. Nothing says the old man can't be happy with me."

"Yeah--like you pulled the trigger," said Terry.

Finch stood up, swung the chair back around, and pushed it under the table. He leaned over and said. "Just one more thing. The rumor mill has it that Charlie wasn't happy about this at all, Captain." He looked straight at Terry. "They've put a price on your head."

Terry looked back at Finch and said, "So what? Lieutenant, when we stepped off the airplane into this war zone, we all got a price on our head."

"Yes, Sir," he answered, "I guess you're right." And he turned to leave.

"Finch!" Terry said. Finch stopped, turned around, and looked back. "Just out of curiosity, how much?"

"Ten thousand bucks, American."

Terry turned to his friend, "Hell—hardly seems worthwhile." And they both laughed.

* * *

He hadn't planned on it, and he didn't think about it consciously, but for some reason that night Terry decided to warm the engine up and do his magneto checks before he taxied out of the revetment. He and Darlington had both put the evening conversation with Finch to rest. It was just going to be another quiet night of mortar watch.

He normally did his engine run-up at the end of the runway, just before takeoff. Tonight while still within the walls of the revetment, he revved up the engine to 1700 RPM, checked the mags, checked the carburetor heat, and throttled back to idle.

Terry stretched his arms out of the windows to pop his back and neck, and then he keyed the intercom mike. "Ready to go, Darlington?"

"Ready," came the reply over the headset.

Terry applied power with the throttle lever in his left hand, taxied out of the revetment and across the PSP ramp to the end of the runway, and swung the tail around so that it was almost touching the barbed wire at the perimeter's edge.

He was just starting to push the throttle lever forward when suddenly he saw a flash of bright orange light out of the corner of his eye and heard an explosion just to his right on the run-up pad where he should have been. And then came another, closer, and to his right rear quarter.

As the adrenaline flowed into his system, time began to slow down. "Take off! *Take off!*" screamed Darlington.

Before he even heard the words, Terry pushed the throttle to full power, and the Bird Dog started to roll. As they began to move forward, there was another explosion right behind them, right where they'd been only moments before.

As they sped down the runway, several more flashes seemed to walk down the runway behind them, just missing them by a couple of yards.

As soon as the wheels came off of the ground, Terry banked hard right and started a maximum performance climb. Darlington was looking to see if he could tell where the mortars were being fired from, but by that time, they'd stopped shooting.

Years later, Terry would tell people, when he would tell people anything at all, that "If I live to be a hundred, which is unlikely for most pilots, I'll never forget the sight of that exploding shell. The flash of orange light suspending the flying particles of shrapnel in mid-flight were like a flash from a camera."

Once they were up and climbing to altitude and in relative safety, Terry keyed his mike. "Darlington, I bet Charlie's mad about missing us that time. Sometimes I think I lead a charmed life. It's like someone's watching out for me. Know what I mean?"

There was silence. Terry turned around to look at his observer, who just smiled and nodded his head.

"Hey, how do you suppose they knew it was me flying tonight, and not one of the other guys?" said Terry.

Darlington thought for a minute, then said "Rockets."

"What do you mean? We all carry rockets, and most of us change them out too," said Terry.

"Yeah, but you're the only one with eight tubes."

"Hey—that may be the answer," said Terry. "When they saw me land and saw all the tubes, they knew whose airplane it was. Smart thinking. So I'm a marked man—or at least my airplane is. You have to wonder, you know? Just think about life and stuff after a near miss like that. Maybe somebody has a plan for me that I don't know about yet. Maybe angels or something. Oh well, where are we supposed to be tonight?"

The little Bird Dog flew on, into the blackness of the jungle night.

* * *

When things were quiet and the flying was routine—and in this case, when the adrenaline had worn off—it became a time for reflection, a time for thinking about things, planning things. Terry's mind would focus on a problem and try to solve it. Or he might work on an invention. Tonight he was thinking about the narrow escape from death. Why had he done his run-up in the revetment instead of on the runway, like he had always done before? Why did he get away with his life when so many of his friends had not?

And then he thought of Ski and Bobby. There had to be another solution to the problem. Every good scrounge that's worth his salt knows that there's always a backup plan. There was always a way to beat the system. Maybe that was why he had been spared this time. What could he do in this case? Like lightning, the answer came to him.

Recon Airplane Company: III Corps, Vietnam

* * *

When Uncle Emery got the letter, he was amazed. All it said was: "Remember Pussyfoot. Main plan failed. Need your help. Please call." Then it gave the name of an army chaplain, his unit, and a Saigon phone number. It was signed "Captain Terry Downey."

Chapter 22

It was a couple of days later when Terry departed Phu Loi. He pointed the nose of the Bird Dog westward toward the big mountain called Nui Ba Den. It would be about a two-hour flight before he arrived at the small town that was located not far from the base of that mountain. The town was called Tay Nghien. He had his overnight bag packed for a three-day stay and was hoping he would draw quarters that had an air conditioner. But he never knew what to expect.

There were two airfields at Tay Nghien. One was called the "downtown strip" because it was literally in the middle of the little town. The other was about five miles away at the big army/air force compound and was the main staging area for III Corps' defensive and offensive activities against the enemy forces that came down the Ho Chi Minh trail through Laos and Cambodia, and then into South Vietnam. The familiar names that described the shape of the river that made up the border were used nightly on the evening news back home in the states—names like "The Parrot's Beak" and "The Angel's Wing." The names were derived from the shapes the river made as it carved the border between South Vietnam and Cambodia.

The company had pilots that flew secret spy missions into Cambodia, searching for enemy activity and supply lines. They'd located major portions of the Ho Chi Minh trail. But politics kept the US from entering those countries in force and interdicting the supply lines and troop movements. The enemy laughed from behind the protected political wall that separated

Recon Airplane Company: III Corps, Vietnam

South Vietnam from its neighbors. Simply put, the US had rules to play by that the enemy did not.

Just north of Tay Nghien, the mountain Nui Ba Den rose majestically from the flat jungle floor. It was an almost perfect cone-shaped mountain, and on the top was a plateau carved by special forces in years past and now manned by an artillery unit. The guns had been flown in by helicopter. Basic military logic says occupy the high ground, and from their vantage point, the 155 mm howitzers could reach targets in a full circle around the mountain for many miles. It was a nice advantage to have. From the top of the mountain, an observer could see for miles which made adjusting the artillery almost as easy as from an aircraft.

Tay Nghien was the home of the Twenty-fifth Division Artillery. When they called for an observer mission, the pilot was sent from his home base flying his Bird Dog. He stayed with the unit for three to five days before returning to base. He ate in their mess hall. He received briefings along with the other officers for daily missions. He usually slept in a bunker inside of the C&C center, or close to it. He had to be ready to go at a moments notice.

Terry had had his own Bird Dog for the last few weeks. It had recently been rebuilt by Cessna Aircraft, and it flew nicely. Normally, when a pilot went to the flight-line, he just got whatever aircraft was next in line. Terry had convinced the CO that they should set up a crew chief system of maintenance—have a single mechanic for a single airplane, with the airplane being flown by one pilot. That way he got to know it inside out. That's how the air force did it. The CO wasn't totally convinced, but he'd agreed to let him do it with one airplane as an experiment.

As soon as Terry had gotten the okay, he'd gone out with the newly assigned crew chief and made some changes. Together they got it cleaned from top to bottom. The underside of the wing was coated with Pentaprime, an oily material that was used to coat gravel runways. Anytime a pilot had to land on a freshly oiled strip, the spinning tires would throw the gunk up onto the underside of the wing. It was largely ignored by maintenance and the pilots. But Terry and the crew chief worked for hours cleaning it off to make it look like new. The primary cleaning ingredient was "wing solvent," a term for the gasoline that could be easily drained from the under-wing sump points and put on a rag. Terry also helped check for loose screws, and he made sure every system was in perfect condition. Then he went to supply and requisitioned four more rocket tubes to add to the four that were already mounted under the wings of the plane. These were mounted in sets of two on the outboard wing shackles. The others were already on the inboard shackles. With the help of his crew chief and the line chief, they put a jack stand under the tail of the airplane and made it sit level. They took a couple pieces of string and taped them on the tubes. It made cross hairs on the front and back of each rocket tube. Then, while the aircraft was jacked up in level flight attitude, he got into the cockpit, picked a point about a half mile away, aligned his body in a normal flight position, and marked the spot on the windshield with a grease pencil. Then they adjusted the rocket tubes so they pointed at the same spot. It was time consuming because they had to adjust the shackle mounting bolts back and forth to achieve the alignment. When they were done, they knew it wasn't perfect, but it was a lot better than before. Eight bore-sighted rocket tubes. Terry was the talk of the company.

Terry's section leader was Capt. Mike Ballard, and he wasn't convinced that this one crew chief-one pilot idea was worth trying. And he didn't like the unconventional look of Terry's airplane, with eight rockets rather than the standard four. But the CO didn't seem to care, so he kept his mouth shut. Mike was a big guy at six-four and nearly 300 pounds. He liked his authority. He used his position to schedule himself as little as possible, and only on the missions he liked. He was an okay pilot, but he lacked finesse. He just didn't have that special ability that allowed a good pilot to get the most out of an airplane when necessary. He didn't have the ability to squeak the airplane on the runway without a bounce and under perfect control.

Terry had the ability that Ballard lacked. And it wasn't some special coordination, because in most other things Terry seemed almost impaired by comparison. He wasn't particularly good at sports, and he couldn't dance well. They often joked that he was "rhythm challenged." But there was something special about flying. In the cockpit things just seemed to work for Terry. His instructors all commented on how quickly he mastered things. Back at Ft. Rucker, during instrument training in the twin-engine Beechcraft Baron, he could identify a dead engine and go through the shutdown procedure faster than anyone. They'd actually tried to get him to slow down. He guessed it had something to do with his mechanical ability. He'd been taking cars and engines apart and putting them back together ever since he was twelve. He considered it his special talent. When that was combined with flying, he guessed it made him aware of what was going on with the airplane and it was like he became a part of the plane.

There were several things to look out for when flying the Tay Nghien mission. Because the border was so close, the enemy could set up anti-aircraft batteries on the other side and shoot into South Vietnam. They had SAM capability, and in places they had radar-controlled .50 caliber machine guns. A missile could often be seen in time for the pilot to take evasive action. The .50 caliber just shot an airplane out of the sky without warning.

Terry had been on station at Tay Nghien two days when they called him for a night flight. There was suspected enemy troop movement about ten klicks south of the city. They wanted him to take an artillery observer up to see if they could spot something, or make the enemy reveal themselves. There was also a report that the enemy had moved some big guns across the border in preparation for the new-year festival they called Tet.

Lt. Carson, called "Kit" by the pilots, had been flying with Terry for the last couple of days, and they were used to each other. He liked Terry's easy-going flying style, and Terry liked his good-natured attitude. Nothing seemed to bother Kit much. He had a job to do, and he did it. But once they were alone in the airplane out over the AO, they made a lot of their own decisions about how to deal with enemy activity. Kit also talked a lot about his frustrations with the system. Forward Observers, as they were known, had a lot of power at their disposal. They could call on air force fighters to do strafing runs and bomb drops. They could call in helicopter gunship teams and medevacs. They could bring artillery batteries to bear anywhere their guns would reach. They could even call on Spooky to tear up the jungle and hopefully the enemy below. Terry's CO often gave his pilots a little lecture about how they had more power in their thumb (the microphone button) than they could ever carry on board. But Terry still liked having his rockets and his M-16, just in case.

Terry and Kit climbed up to about 3,000 feet that night and started patrolling the AO. Things seemed real quiet. Kit started talking about the troubles he was having getting fire into enemy locations. "Every time I find Charlie," he said over the intercom, "I call in a fire mission and have to wait over fifteen minutes to get clearance. And then they won't fire at the spot I tell them to. I call them with the target, they call HQ for permission, HQ calls the province chief for permission, and he says no, but you can shoot three grid squares over. It's frustrating, to say the least. One day we snuck up on an undiscovered base camp. They didn't see us, and we marked their location good. We set up an arc light for that night. By the time the clearances came down, the B-52s ended up dropping their load three miles away, but the province chief probably warned the base camp just in case and they moved out, and we never did find 'em again." He was animated as he talked. Terry could feel his frustration.

The conversation notwithstanding, Terry was feeling good that night. The air was smooth and the airplane was running great. "How about a little fun?" he asked.

"What you got in mind?" Kit replied.

"Have you ever done any aerobatics?" Terry asked with a chuckle.

"Go ahead—anything to break the monotony."

Terry had been practicing a lot, mostly while flying the Lerps. He had a lot of time to kill, so why not practice his pilot skills? As long as he kept positive G-forces on the aircraft, there was no harm done. His favorite so far was the barrel roll. He started a shallow dive to the left to build up airspeed. "Hang on," he said. Then he gently but firmly pulled back the stick and pushed it firmly to the right. It didn't respond like a fighter plane, but it went over nice and easy. When he was fully inverted, he put a little forward pressure on the stick to keep it from falling into a split S, then it gently rolled back to normal straight and level flight.

"Nice," said Kit. "I hardly felt a thing. Kinda funny seeing the city lights through the overhead windows though. Let's fly over toward the border now, and see what we can see."

Terry could tell by his voice that "upside-down" made him a little nervous, so he held the airplane level and then gently turned south toward the river that formed the border between Cambodia and South Vietnam. They'd been flying level for about twenty minutes when Terry heard it—"beep-beep," a short burst over the FM radio. The adrenaline shot through his system, and without a moment's thought he pushed the stick hard right and they were rolling upside-down again. But this time when he got to the fully inverted position, he pulled back on the stick and cut the throttle, and pointed the nose straight at the ground. He caught sight of the tracers going past his right wing out of the corner of his eye as they dove for the deck.

"Youch! What is this all about?" said Kit in a surprised voice as his body started to feel the Gs.

Terry was too busy to answer. He started a gentle pull out of the dive when he saw the needle on the airspeed indicator get close to the red line. It went five knots past the line before they finally leveled off at 500 feet, with the airplane pointed back toward the lights of the city. "Radar-controlled fifty," he finally said, catching his breath. "We pulled a few Gs on that maneuver. You can thank Capt. Bob Richards that we're still alive."

"Who's that?" Kit asked.

"He was one of my instructors back in flight school. He survived a hit from a radar-controlled fifty cal. The sound in the radio was just like he described. All I could do was try to dive out before they got a lock on. I saw tracers, but I don't think they hit us. We'll check it out when we get on the ground."

Kit called into base and reported the near miss. They told them that a Cobra gunship had seen the tracers coming up at them and had marked their location. They were inside the border, which made them fair game, and they were going after them. Two other Cobras had been called in to help and were on the way.

They stayed a little ways out of the area and climbed back to 4,000 feet. Terry felt that would put them pretty much out of range, and they would see if they could help spot. Then as they watched, they saw it. Red streaks came out of the ground into the sky in front of them, then another burst of red. Then out of a black space in the sky, a stream of red so intense that it looked like a small river headed toward the spot on the ground from where the fifty was firing. The Cobra had found his target. After another burst from the ground, the Cobra pumped another red stream at the target, only this time from a lower altitude. Terry couldn't see the Cobra, but he knew that it was diving on the target. There were two more short bursts from the ground, then another steady stream from the sky, and then nothing.

The other two Cobras joined the first, and they did a good job of shooting up the whole area. No more fire came from the ground.

"You see that, Kit?" Terry asked.

"Sure did. I hope the chopper made it through that firestorm."

They monitored the radios and were relieved to hear that all three Cobras made it back to base. They flew the Bird back to base about an hour later and once on the ground and safely at the TOC, they wrote up their after-action report. "Well, that's one that didn't get away. No province chief to stop us when we're under fire," Terry said to Kit.

* * *

The next day they were back in the air. They flew over the area where the firefight had occurred. They knew exactly where the Cobras had been working, but below them was dense jungle. It still looked about the same. They'd be sending ground troops into the area to see if they could find equipment or bodies, but this was almost always futile. All they usually found were a few trails of blood where Charlie had dragged his people out.

In the evenings in their lounge back at Phu Loi, the pilots talked about these missions they flew. Separately, they never made a lot of sense. When you put them together, sometimes a pattern emerged. Terry told them about Kit's comments about getting fire clearance, and they told similar stories. None of them could really understand why. But they were raised with certain knowledge, a firsthand knowledge of freedom. They thought most everybody understood that basic concept. They thought that maybe their efforts would make a difference for these people. Maybe their assumptions were wrong.

Tim Ewell

* * *

About three days later, Capt. Ballard took Terry's airplane on a mission. He came back that night and had the crew chief take off the extra rocket tubes. Terry was spitting mad. "Too heavy," Ballard said. "Could hardly make a good turn. Won't pull out of a steep dive." Terry felt like saying something about the fact that Ballard's fat ass outweighed him by almost 130 pounds, but for once he kept his mouth shut. It was good while it had lasted. Ballard killed the idea of the individual crew chief too. Terry didn't get to fly his special airplane much after that. It was the nicest airplane in the company because he had worked very hard to make it that way. Ballard made it his favorite aircraft. It became his aircraft of choice, and he got his choice a lot. Before long it got dirty and became just like all the others—functional, but nothing special.

Chapter 23

Ski arranged for Bobby to return to the orphanage. Terry was now the company's head scrounge, and he also got part of Pop's money-changing secret. Pop agreed to give him half of the net proceeds to keep it going for as long as Terry was still in country. His only stipulation was that he couldn't hand it off when he left. Pop would arrange the next transfer—or not, depending on how secure he was feeling at the time. Pop trusted Terry, and that was big, but he still kept his hand on the pulse to make sure it all stayed as risk-free as possible. Not even Ski or Hank knew about the money thing. They thought the Beaver was just about Bobby.

Ski only had four months left before his DEROS. He wrote letters home to Barbara every day. He was grasping at straws. They were going back to try the adoption angles again, but that seemed hopeless.

It was about a month later, and the swimming pool was nearing completion. The rebar was in place, and the cement had been scrounged. They would be doing the pour in about a week. Saunders, of all people, had scrounged up a pump and filter system that he'd found at an abandoned airfield. It had been part of their water supply system. He told Terry about it, and together they'd gotten the lieutenant at the engineer company to lend them a couple of guys and some tools. They used the trusty old Beaver to fly out and retrieve the parts, along with quite a bit of pipe.

At this point in time, there was only one officer who was adamant about what he called the "foolishness and waste of the pool project." That was the lazy, fat-ass, overweight, Capt. "Bastard." He'd even called up to headquarters to complain, but had gotten no response. He would just wait and see what happened when the new CO came in, and that was due to happen in the next two weeks. "There'll be hell to pay if I have to help haul concrete to build that thing," he complained to anyone who would listen. All the other pilots had noticed how he had been conspicuously absent during any time of manual labor. His large girth made him more prone to sweating than the others, and he just did not like to sweat. This earned him another nickname—"Sweaty"—which was used when he wasn't around. The pilots could use either or both when referring to him, and everyone would know who they were talking about.

Unknown to most of the loyal pilot laborers, there were a few who sided with Sweaty. They didn't like the extra work, and they didn't have the vision to picture what it would be like when it was completed. Sweaty started working that to his advantage and tried to undermine the day-to-day efforts. He had a plan of his own. He just needed a few of them to side with him at the right time, and then it would all be over.

The next week came and went. Thanks to Sweaty's interference, the concrete was no closer to being poured than a week earlier, and now they were preparing for the departure of Maj. Pratt and the introduction of the new CO, whoever that might be.

It was on the night before he was to leave that Major Pratt sent for Terry. It was after seven that evening when Terry finished his mission and arrived at the door to the CO's office. He knocked, and a voice called out, "Enter."

The outer office was empty, the company first sergeant's desk unoccupied. "In here," the voice said from beyond the next door.

Terry stepped into the CO's private office, stepped up to the desk where Pratt was seated, snapped to attention, and saluted smartly. "Capt. Downey, reporting as ordered, Sir."

"At ease, Terry. It's just you and me, and I want this informal."

Terry relaxed his stance. "No problem, Sir. What can I do for you?"

Major Pratt got up from his desk and motioned to the two chairs at the side of the room. "Come on over and sit down. I want to share some things with you," he said.

The major walked over to a small fridge in the corner and pulled out two bottles of Budweiser, popped the cap on both of them, and walked over and handed one to Terry.

"Thanks," said Terry, and he took a small swig from the bottle.

The major began. "Terry, I just wanted to thank you for taking on the project I gave you. You have exceeded my expectations. When it gets done—if it gets done—it will be a great place to cool off and relax."

"What do you mean, "if"? asked Terry.

"It's like this. The guy who is coming in to take my place is a headquarters-type who needs command time to punch his card for promotion. He has little or no experience in actual command. The old man gave him his pick of commands. That's a sure sign he's a real kiss-ass. He chose this company because of its excellent record of accomplishment and team morale. Now listen carefully. I've already heard the rumor that your nemesis, Captain Ballard, is plotting to stop completion of the pool."

"Uh, why would anyone let that happen?" asked Terry.

"Terry, one of the reasons I like you is that you're a lot like I used to be. You have ambition, and you know how to work things to your advantage. I've been there before myself, and I still find that it can make needed things happen when I need them to. That's what the pool was all about. When you go back to the world, check out that movie I told you about. It will explain a lot."

"But what can Sweaty—I mean, Capt. Ballard do to stop it? We have everything we need. I'm sorry it wasn't finished before you left, but you have my word that I'll see to it—and it'll have water in it in less than a month."

"You can't promise that, Terry. What if Ballard convinces the new CO to stop the work?"

Terry had never even considered the possibility, and it took him by surprise. "What do you suggest . . . should I—"

The CO put up his hand. "Terry, listen to me. Top and I are good friends. We served together before, and when you're friends with your first sergeant, you can accomplish more than if you're friends with a dozen wannabe officers. I gave him some discreet direction to help you out. You'll have to keep that secret between the three of us. Get with him after I leave, and you can solve the problem, if it needs to be solved. I hope it doesn't come to that, but if it does . . . well, let's just say that it's NCOs who get the real work done, and Top knows how to make it happen."

"But—"

"Terry, that's all you need for now. Go to the club and have another beer. I'm being assigned to the Pentagon, and my promotion to Lt. Colonel isn't far off. Let's just say you won't be forgotten. Close the door on your way out."

Terry stood up and walked to the door. Then he turned and saluted the man who was now his silent mentor. Major Pratt saluted back.

* * *

Ah, the complexities of a good plan, Terry thought as he walked toward the O Club. *But it might just be the angle I need for the bigger plan.* He could hear Pop's voice echoing in his head. *Terry, remember the rules. Number one, don't get caught. Rule one alpha, if you get caught, blame the Aussies.*

Damn, he'd almost forgotten about the Aussies. The Australian presence in country was small, but they had a great reputation—and Pop had taught him how to capitalize on it.

* * *

Just as the CO predicted, the day after his departure, Major Dumbshit, known officially as Major Skiles, ordered all work on the pool to stop. Sweaty and a couple of his sidekicks had paid him a visit, and they'd convinced him that the pool was a boondoggle. Terry had not expected it to happen so quickly. He'd thought he'd have time to develop a contingency plan, but now he didn't have the luxury of time. And haste could lead to mistakes. He needed help. All this, and he was just about to let Ski know that his own special plan for Bobby was finally coming together.

Terry decided to give the new CO the benefit of the doubt and see if he'd listen to reason. He told the first sergeant he needed to see the old man some time that day. Top had told him his schedule was full and that he could set him up for 1500 hours the following day. Terry agreed. Once again he was back on the walk from the head shed to his quarters. He met Ski on the way.

"Hey" said Terry. "Got a minute?"

"On my way to operations to pick my stuff for my mission. A minute's all I got," said Ski.

"Tonight, 1900, my place. Bring Hank. I got something for you."

"Wow, what's the big secret?"

"Can't tell you now," said Terry. "Be there?"

"Yeah, okay. Well, let's think about that. Uh, where else do I have to be—the opera?"

"Funny you should say that, 'cause we need to make a fat lady sing," said Terry with a chuckle.

"Get *outta* here. I gotta go. See you tonight." Ski turned and walked toward the ops bunker.

As Terry approached the O Club and the pool site, he heard an argument. Two officers were exchanging heated words. Both held a can of beer and took a drink in between exchanges.

"You know what?" said Saunders. "You sided with Sweaty and stopped it. I have another six months to go in this swamp, and a swimming pool would have been a nice place to cool off."

"I really don't give a shit what you think is nice, Lieutenant," said Capt. Jensen. "I for one am tired of working on this useless fucking project. You want me to show you what this hole is good for? I'll show you—" and he threw his empty beer can in the hole that was to have been the pool.

"And I thought Sweaty Bastard was the bad guy. You're as much a lazy ass as he is." Saunders turned to walk away, but Jensen caught his shoulder. "Take your hand off of me," said Saunders firmly. "Go take up your issues with someone else."

Jensen saw the look in Saunders' eyes and let go. He didn't want to mess with the big lieutenant. "Just watch your tongue, Lieutenant," he said, then he turned and walked away.

Saunders saw Terry approaching. "Hey, how ya doin." he said to Terry as his adrenaline started to subside.

"Bill, listen—don't let this get to you. I'm going to talk to the new CO and see if I can get us back on track. Remember—*illegitimus non carbarundum*." Don't let the bastards grind you down—and in this case, one particular bastard.

In the club, Terry watched the other officers as the evening progressed. They were back in their sullen do–nothing-but-drink mode. As they left the club, one after the other would toss an empty beer can into the hole, as if it were a ritual. Terry was pissed, but he held his tongue. It wouldn't do any good making enemies of his friends. Major Pratt had been the bad guy on this deal, and Terry had just been his worker bee. He only got the side-effects from the anger. If he became the defender of the pool, then he would become the bad guy. Pop had taught him better than that.

Chapter 24

There they were again, the special ops planners back in their planning room. Terry's AC unit was working pretty well, and with the door closed, it was pretty cool. Hank was puzzled as to why he'd been called. Pussyfoot was over. They'd tried and failed.

"Ski," said Terry cautiously, "I don't want to get you hopes up, but I have some possible good news for you. Hank, as always, we need your sage advice. The last plan failed not because we didn't have it figured out, but because an unseen force jumped up and grabbed us."

"What in the hell are you talking about?" said Ski.

"I have another way to get Bobby out."

Ski's face took on a look of astonishment and disbelief, with a trace of hope. But he wasn't prepared to go through all this again. "What did you do, find another Beaver?" he said.

"Terry," said Hank, "if you have something that has potential, I'll listen. Otherwise, I'm outta here." He turned to Ski and said, "Give him a couple of minutes, then we'll go get a drink."

"Thanks for the confidence," said Terry.

The other two just shrugged, as if to say, it ain't gonna happen.

"Okay, here's the deal," Terry began. "Remember my Uncle Emery I told you about? I wrote to him. He agreed to help. I gave him an assignment . . . and he came through. I really didn't think it was possible either. I asked him to find a flight crew on one of the 707s that take us in and out of country. It had to be a flight crew that we could trust and would stick their necks out just a little bit for a good cause."

"So you're going to put him on the jump seat or something?" asked Hank.

"Not exactly," replied Terry, "but close." As he explained the plan, he saw real hope return to Ski's face. It was worth waiting for. "Now I need a couple of favors from you," he added after finishing the details. "They involve Sweaty and the pool. Will you help?"

They nodded cautiously, knowing how wild some of the plans were that came out of their tight-knit little group.

"I invited Saunders to join us. Is that okay with you?"

"Sure," Ski said for all of them. "But why?"

"Give me a minute and I'll explain it all," said Terry. He opened up the door and saw Saunders walking down the hall. He motioned him over and asked him to join them.

"Okay—here's the deal," Terry said when Saunders took a seat. "I've just about had it with Sweaty. Does anybody here think he is a good officer?"

The other three all shook their heads.

"Anybody mind if we take him down a couple of notches?"

"Get me alone with him and I'll take him down a couple all by myself," said Saunders.

"That's not what I mean," said Terry. "But I promise you it will be fun to watch."

"What does this have to do with Bobby?" asked Ski.

"It's all part of the same thing. The Aussies need a favor. We're going to take care of that for them. They're going to give us a favor. Sweaty needs some exercise, and we need the pool finished. Wouldn't it be nice if he volunteered?"

"Terry, why is everything so complicated with you?" asked Hank.

"This is pretty simple, really," said Terry. "What would it take to get Sweaty to volunteer to work on the pool? Maybe to get out of a court martial?"

"Hell. What has he done to deserve that?" said Saunders.

"I think he stole something from the Aussies and they're going to press charges," replied Terry.

"What in the hell are you talking about?"

"Remember that pistol he had that he said was stolen?" Everyone nodded. "Would it surprise you to know that he's been acquiring pistols that he intends to ship home when he leaves in two months? He really has a good plan on how to get them back. I was amazed that he had the brains. But he made the mistake of telling someone he trusted who told someone else who told me."

"Go on," said Ski.

"Okay—I have a way for them to be discovered and make him a candidate for a court-martial. His way out will be to reinstate the pool project and set an example for his friends by volunteering to do all the grunt work."

"Hey, if he figures out who finked on him, it'll put us in a lot of risk," said Hank cautiously.

"Leave that part to me," said Terry. "I just need two of you to move a couple of boxes from one place to another and replace them with special ones that I'll show you. Then just forget about it and watch it happen. Can I count on you for that?"

They looked at one another and all of them nodded. Saunders got a huge grin on his face. "You pull this off and you'll never have to buy another beer."

Chapter 25

A special tall metal box had been delivered to the convent, accompanied by a letter of instructions. It explained how they were to help a young boy named Bobby get used to being inside it. The box came with a special teddy bear. They told Bobby it was to be his special hiding place. It took some getting used to, but after a while it wasn't too bad. Whenever he was in the box, they gave him the teddy bear, and he loved that bear. He of all people knew about the need to hide. The sisters would play games with him while he was in the box. Because it had rollers on the bottom, they would roll it around on the floor. He got used to the game, and sometimes even fell asleep while they were playing.

* * *

Terry flew the Bird Dog, and Ski sat in the back holding Bobby on his lap. The flight from Phu Loi to Tan Son Nhut only took about forty-five minutes. They taxied down to the air force's FAC shack at the end of Charlie Row. True to his word, Lt. Don Moss was waiting there for him with his Jeep and driver. Nobody messed with Don, not even MPs, so when they got to the transport location, they just drove through like they owned the place. There was one building where the food was prepared for the big transport aircraft that brought the troops in and out of country. It was a bit out of the way, and that was perfect for their situation.

Don let them off and pointed to the door. A very attractive dark-haired woman, about thirty years old and dressed in a flight attendant's uniform, was standing just inside, holding the door partway open. She smiled, looked around cautiously, and motioned for them to come in. When they got inside, they found they were in a small side storage room, and in the center of the room was that special metal box that Bobby had become very familiar with. He saw the special mark of the kangaroo stenciled on the side.

Chapter 26

The boarding area for the soldiers departing country was filled with GIs of every branch and rank. There were army, air force, and marines. There were colonels and privates, and everything in between. Most were sitting down in one of the parallel rows of chairs lined up back to back across the room. Most held a few special carry-on items or souvenirs from their one year tour of duty in their laps. Some were standing in small groups, sharing experiences. Some told of hopes and dreams about what they were going to do when they finally got back to the states, what they called "The World." The area itself was just a simple structure facing the flight line of the Bien Hoa airfield. It just had a tin roof with pole supports, and the walls were see-through mosquito netting. MPs stood at strategic points around the room and guarded the entry and exit to assure that only those with legitimate orders would be allowed to board the Big Bird home.

Out on the ramp in front, the service crew was busy readying the Boeing 707 for the long flight to Travis Air Force Base. It was another contract flight by Flying Tigers. There were three stops planned in the fourteen-plus-hour flight—the Philippines, Wake Island, and Hawaii. The Pacific Ocean is a big stretch of water. Bags were being loaded and fuel trucks were pumping jet fuel into the tanks. Other ground crew were checking this and that to make sure all was in order.

The last vehicle to drive up to the plane was the food service catering truck. Armanski and Terry watched from the cockpit of the Bird Dog parked on the ramp adjacent to the 707. The

Tim Ewell

catering truck scissor-lift hoisted the rear body of its truck up to the service door on the plane. *So far, so good*, he thought, but his heart was racing and there was a small knot in his stomach. Bobby sat on a pillow inside the specially prepared container aboard the catering truck. It looked just like any other meal container, but its cargo was much more precious.

Inside the box it was dark, but Bobby knew what he had to do. Just sit and wait. Someone would get him out soon. He felt the elevator lift come to a stop, and someone took hold of his hiding place and wheeled it across the ramp and into the airplane. He heard voices but remembered what Ski and the sisters had said. "Stay still and be quiet." And he was going to do just that.

Aboard the aircraft, two MPs stood at the main door, occasionally turning around to check the activity of the catering crew, but mostly talking to each other about their upcoming schedules. The special cart was wheeled into place and locked down next to the others. When all the food carts were in place, one of the workers called to the MPs and said, "Loaded! We're on our way out." One of the MPs turned toward the voice, nodded, and went back to his conversation. A stewardess closed the service door behind them as the service crew left.

The cockpit door opened and a tall uniformed figure appeared. The three stripes on his sleeve identified him as the copilot. He glanced toward the open entry door where the MPs stood. He walked over to the stewardess, who was still in the galley. "Everything okay?" he said softly.

She nodded and pointed to the roll-on container safely tucked into the wall. He saw the little kangaroo stenciled on the top. He turned back and walked over to the two MPs. "We're ready whenever you are," he said.

"Right, Sir!" came the reply from the senior MP as he reached for his two-way radio to inform the dispatcher that they were ready for boarding. Boarding took about thirty minutes, and the stewardess was a little concerned about her cargo. She pulled out the cart a little way and opened the top to allow a peek. Then she closed it again and slid it back in its place.

The airplane was on takeoff roll, and every seat was filled with service men returning home. Many of the men were dressed in Class A uniforms. Some were still in jungle fatigues. To the lead stewardess, it created a visual patchwork of color as she looked over the seats from the front to the back of the aircraft. They all sat in hushed silence as the nose of the airplane lifted into the air and the wheels left the runway. The sound of the landing gear being retracted brought a couple of whispers, but when it thunked as it locked in the up position, a cheer erupted and applause sounded for about two minutes. They were finally on their way out of what many felt was a true hell—and they were glad.

Bobby had been sitting in the blackness of his container for over an hour and had grown sleepy and drifted off. The cheers and applause woke him, and for a couple of seconds he forgot where he was and began to cry. By the time the applause stopped, he remembered his special mission and what the sisters had told him, and he snuggled his teddy bear close and quieted down again. The thunderous applause and the roar of the jet engines had masked his crying. He waited patiently in the darkness. He'd done this before, when he had to hide in the secret tunnel with the sisters and the other kids at the orphanage, but when he was in the tunnel the others were always there. This time he was alone.

In another forty-five minutes they reached 33,000 feet and leveled off. The stewardesses were busy with coffee and juice and preparing for the first meal service when the copilot came out again from the cockpit. He walked the few steps back to the galley and found Jill. "Let's do it!" he said, glancing around the immediate area. Everyone seemed pretty preoccupied with things around them. This would be the perfect time for the switch.

Bobby felt his cart start to roll as the stewardess and the copilot pulled it out and wheeled it into the cockpit. When the door to the cockpit was securely closed and locked behind them, they opened the top of the container.

Bright sunlight from the cockpit windows shone in and Bobby squinted as he looked out at the three faces that looked down on him. "Come on, young man," said the copilot as he reached in and carefully lifted the little boy outs. Bobby was still clutching his brown-and-white teddy bear as he rose into the arms of the stranger. "Boy, you must be special. Somebody called in a lot of favors to get you here."

"Special—he's adorable," said Jill, the dark-haired stewardess. She put out her hands and Bobby stretched his out toward her. Her dark uniform looked a lot like a nun's habit, except for the short skirt. Bobby had never seen a short skirt like that before, but it only distracted him for a moment. Then he put his arms around her, and she held him like he was her own child. He felt the warmth and the love, and he was once again at peace—even in this very strange place.

Bobby didn't understand it all, but he was glad to be out of the box. He looked around at the funny room with all the knobs and dials.

The captain turned back around in his seat and said, "Well, make our stowaway comfortable and get back to work. It's still a long way to the Philippines." And then he reached over to make some adjustments to his radio volume and then the throttles.

At each stop, they had to make sure that Bobby was back in his box, and that the service crew did not try to remove it from the airplane. When they finally arrived at Travis AFB, near Sacramento, they told him that he would have to be very quiet, and that it would be a bit longer before he could get out of his container. His cart was unloaded with the rest of the food service carts into the elevator truck, then driven to the service area. When his box was finally opened, he found himself in a back room, and the first thing he saw was familiar—a tall, lanky man dressed in a uniform, with a big Texas cowboy hat.

Pop lifted him from the container and stood him on his feet. "Well," he said, "looks like we both made it after all. Are you ready to meet your new mommy?" He took him by the hand and, like he owned the place, walked right out through the main section of the food service area and out into the waiting area, where a mix of soldiers and families were greeting each other with a lot of emotion. He pushed open the glass doors at the front of the building and walked out into the sunshine to the parking lot.

Standing beside a green 1967 Chevrolet was an attractive blond woman. She looked nervous. Bobby reached over and held onto Pop's leg. Barbara knelt down and whispered his name quietly. "Bobby?"

Pop took Bobby's hand and guided him over to Barbara. She couldn't help it—she started to cry. It was just a little sob, but her eyes filled with tears. Bobby put his hand out and touched her face. She smiled and caught her breath. They looked at each other. "He *is* beautiful, just like Steve told me," she said, looking up at Pop.

Bobby looked up at Pop and said in broken English, "This my mommy?"

That was it, the tears were full blown now. She grabbed him and held him and said, "Yes, yes—" and then she remembered and said, "Oui, oui!"

"This is just too much emotion," said Pop as he choked back tears. "I am an officer and a gentleman—at least that's what they tell me, and I don't get emotional."

That elicited laughter. They got in the car and drove off base. They both had tickets from San Francisco. Barbara was going back to Dothan, and Pop was headed to his duty station. He wouldn't be there for long because he'd volunteered for another tour in 'Nam. After all, he had a business to run, and Stick was not about to let him off the hook when the deal was almost done.

* * *

Back in Phu Loi, Terry had taken Major Pratt's advice and met with the first sergeant. An inspection had been arranged, and the contents of a certain box had been discovered. The box, with the kangaroo stenciled on the side, had been claimed by Capt. Mike Ballard. When the first sergeant called the MPs and the Aussie commander, Capt. Ballard, alias Sweaty Bastard, had not only confessed, he'd begged for a deal. The new CO of the Eighty-ninth was caught at a loss. He didn't want a black mark on his record. He'd shown support for Sweaty, and now he had to distance himself or answer a lot of questions from his boss at Battalion HQ. The first sergeant subtly suggested that he reverse his position on the pool to show the company—and Battalion—that he wasn't part of the weapons conspiracy that had trapped Sweaty. And why not let Sweaty really sweat and be allowed to do the majority of the manual labor on the pool?

They struck a deal with Sweaty that avoided a court–martial, and he was happy to get off so easy. Saunders laughed to himself as he watched him carrying cement and concrete bags, one by one, from the front of the company area back to the pool. Most of the other guys just cut him off and wouldn't have anything to do with him. The CO took him out of his leadership position and assigned him to full-time pool construction. He had to do whatever Saunders told him to do.

It was good to know that once in a while, justice was done. Two days before he left country, Terry was given the honor of being the first to dive in the newly filled pool. Then they all jumped in. There were a lot of proud officers that day. They were proud of their accomplishment and proud of their friends.

Chapter 26

The announcement, in big capital letters, read: TWENTY-FIRST BIRTHDAY PARTY.

There were only five who made the trip to Dallas to the home of Col. Steve and Barbara Armanski. Pop Danforth flew in from his retirement home in Miami in his own airplane, a Cessna Citation jet. Terry and his wife came on an airline from Olympia, Washington. Saunders drove up from San Antonio, and Sergeant Hull—Puck—flew in from Long Beach, California.

Only Hank was missing. He was shot down in 1969 over Xuan Loc. He came home on a special C-130 and was buried in his home town in Alabama.

The Armanski home was decorated with banners and photographs. Music from the sixties was playing on the stereo. On the fireplace mantle were family photos of Steve and Barbara holding Bobby. And there was a picture of the twin girls. Seems the doctor had been wrong. Just six months after Steve got back from his tour in Vietnam, Barbara announced the miracle. Bobby, who was now speaking pretty good English, was told he would have a sibling. Bobby seemed happy and looked up at his mom and said, "When will Pop bring him here?"

But today Bobby was the birthday boy. Not only that, he'd just last month graduated from Texas A&M, summa cum laude. Thanks to his amazing heritage, he was nearly six foot tall, and he still spoke French, although his Vietnamese had pretty much faded.

Sometimes it's a good thing that when you grow up you can remember things from when you were six. For Bobby it was good that he remembered life before this family. He remembered the orphanage, and he remembered his escape. He barely remembered his birth mother and father. Given the circumstances, that wasn't such a bad thing. It was explained to him early on why he couldn't talk to others about his adventure, and because he was unusually bright and compliant, the secret never came out. It never would. Today he was just another bright American boy with an American birth certificate who could one day become president, if that was his dream.

After they cut the cake, and after most everyone had called it a night, one old bold pilot and two middle-aged pilots and one gray-haired radio operator sat in the living room, reliving the war days. They recounted the stories of how they'd been spit upon and jeered at and called baby killers when they came home. Here in this group of four it was safe to express the truth. It had come out in later years how Hull had been one of Pop's secret operatives, and that was the real reason he kept his mouth shut when all the unusual and unauthorized activity was taking place. There were probably still some secrets out there that Pop had held close, and only he would know the whole story.

They'd all gone their own way since then. But they had this one thing in common. They'd found a way to find something good in an unpopular war. It was something no one could take away from them, even though they could never tell anyone about it. It was their special good feeling.

"A toast," said Terry, raising his glass. "To those we lost, the ones who tried their best and gave it all for the country they loved—and for the friends they cherished."

They touched glasses and in unison said, "Hear, hear."

Afterword

My son Alex came to me one evening while I was reading my newspaper in the living room. He was fourteen at the time and in the eighth grade. We'd finished eating dinner, and for a change we'd all been together, one of those rare times in those busy days of teenagers and work schedules. I was feeling quite relaxed and comfortable. Over dinner we'd discussed Alex's plans to go with his classmates on their civics trip to visit Washington DC, a major trip from California to the East Coast. It would be quite an adventure.

He came up beside my chair and said, "Dad?"

I looked over my paper and said, "What is it, Al?" I wasn't paying much attention, but something in his voice said he had an important question.

"I've just been thinking, Dad. Would you like me to get you a rubbing from the wall?"

My attention shifted from the article I'd been reading, and my heart did a little flip. It felt like a weight had just been placed on the core of my soul. I looked at Alex and put my paper down on my lap. I knew exactly what he was talking about, and a harsh reality that I'd been suppressing for nearly twenty years caused my words to stick in my throat.

To Alex, it seemed that I was angry that he'd asked the question. All he wanted to do was a special favor for his dad—to bring him back a rubbing of the name of a friend from the Vietnam Memorial there in DC. But when he asked the question, he saw my face fall. And although I looked right at him, I couldn't speak.

I tried to say something, but somehow the words just wouldn't come out. Alex, puzzled and a little hurt by my response said, "Sorry," and turned and went to his room.

I didn't mean to react that way. It was just something that happened. For several minutes I could only think of a few special people whose friendships were short. They were friends who shared a common bond of duty, honor, country—but most of all, a love for flying.

After sitting in silence for several minute and gathering my thoughts and emotions, I went into the kitchen where I had a small desk. I took out a plain piece of paper and wrote down two names: Captain Mike Hope and Lieutenant Tom DePalma. There were others I could have written down, but these were good examples of a lifetime of memories that took place in just one year as a Reconnaissance Airplane Pilot in Vietnam. I felt relieved just to have written the names down. I carried it into Alex's room and saw him lying face down on his bed.

"Can I talk to you for a minute?" I asked.

"Sorry, Dad. I didn't mean to upset you."

"You didn't upset me," I replied, "you just surprised me. I hadn't thought about some of those people in a long time. Here." I handed him the paper bearing the two names, the two memories, the two lives that were no more. "These are two special names, and I would really appreciate it if you could get a rubbing for me from the wall."

"Sure, Dad? Are you sure you want me to?" he said, cautious excitement in his voice.

"I'm sure," I replied, and I gave him a big hug. He couldn't really understand, but I could tell he tried to. I went back my chair. I sat down and tears filled my eyes. *Why now?* I thought. *Why twenty years later? Why didn't I cry then?*

After Alex got back from his trip to the capital and had unpacked all of his dirty laundry and the souvenirs he'd purchased on his trip, he came out of his room to where I was sitting in the living room, in my favorite chair. "I brought you something from DC, Dad." And he handed me a single sheet of paper. It was small, about three by eight inches, and rubbed into the surface with a pencil was the name "Michael Hope."

I thanked Alex. "I wish I could tell you all that this means to me," I said.

I sat and studied it for some time. Quietly, reflectively, I remembered the man that was the name, the man who was his own special legend in his own special domain in Xuan Loc, Vietnam. I remembered how he lived and how he died. All of us pilots who knew him knew he would probably die there. We felt that it was the way he wanted it.

In my memory, in that piece of pencil-rubbed paper, in that name engraved in black marble, he lives on, probably not forever, but maybe long enough to tell his story and the story of a few other people who lived and died in a far away place, in another time. It felt like a much different world then.

From that feeling, it became my mission to somehow memorialize the story of a number of gentlemen with whom I served. Just writing the book was a catharsis for me. A lot of healing has taken place within my soul by virtue of the remembrances.

A lot of what's written in this story has a firm basis in truth. Of course all of the names have been changed, and the story line is a combination of fact and fiction. But many of the characters are loosely based on people I knew. Some I appreciated greatly because they got me through a really tough time in my life, and I'm honored to call them friends.

Glossary

ADIZ   Air Defense Identification Zone

ADF   Automatic Direction Finder A realitively crude radio system that allowed an operator to "home in" on a signal from the antenna generating it.

AFVN   Armed Forces Vietnam Radio A radio station set up by the military to give limited news and information and some entertainment and music for the troops who had radios.

AO   Area of Operations

DEROS   Date Eligible for Return from Over Seas

FO   Forward Observer

HE   High Explosive

LRRP   Long Range Reconnaissance Patrol. Pronounced lerp. A team of soldiers, usually 8 to 14, who would be inserted into the battlefield to search for enemy activity. They would spend from several day to several weeks in their operations area until extracted.

LZ   Landing Zone. It was a place where a helicopter could land to drop off or pick up men and equipment. It was usually just an open, level spot on the terrain.

MAG   Magneto. The system that supplies electrical charge to the spark plugs on most standard aircraft engines.

Medivac   A Slick (see Slick below) that has been outfitted with stretchers and medical equipment for transport of the wounded. When a medivac was not available, any slick would do.

MSL   Mean Sea Level (Mean height of the ocean)

Nails   A nickname for a Flechette. In the case of a rocket it was the warhead which contained hundreds of small steel darts that would fly toward the target in a large swath.

Nomex   A special fire retardant material used for the making of flight suits and pilots gloves.

NVA   The regular North Vietnam Army

Point Man   The member of a team who takes the lead when traversing terrain. In Vietnam they had a short life expectancy because they were the ones who would first encounter trip wires and land mines. Even a careful point man could miss a carefully concealed wire or step on a buried mine.

RAC   Reconnaissance Airplane Company

RPG   Rifle Propelled Grenade

RTO   Radio Telephone Operator (Radio operator

SAM   Surface to Air Missile

Satchel   Generally, just a bag or other container of explosives which are set to go off when disturbed by motion or by pulling an attached string.

Slick   A Huey Helicopter without mounted guns or rockets used mainly for troop transport.

Specialist   Spec is short for Specialist, an army grade that at the time went up in grade from Spec 4. A spec 4 is equivalent in pay grade to a Corporal. But whereas a Corporal had command authority to give orders to those in rank below that grade, a Specialist had no such authority to command or give orders.

TDY   Temporary Duty

TO&E   Table of Organization and Equipment. The list of personnel and equipment needed and authorized for each unit.

TOC   Tactical Operations Center

VC   Vietcong. The revolutionary soldiers of the indigenous population.

Vulcan Cannon   A 7.62MM automatic gun with a series of rotating barrels that fires two to three thousand rounds per minute.

www.ingramcontent.com/pod-product-compliance
Lightning Source LLC
LaVergne TN
LVHW091533070526
838199LV00001B/48